Kerala
KALEIDOSCOPE

RESPLENDENT RECOLLECTIONS OF A BYGONE ERA

T N VENUGOPALAN

BLUEROSE PUBLISHERS
India | U.K.

Copyright © T N Venugopalan 2024

All rights reserved by author. No part of this publication may be reproduced, stored in a retrieval system or transmitted in any form or by any means, electronic, mechanical, photocopying, recording or otherwise, without the prior permission of the author. Although every precaution has been taken to verify the accuracy of the information contained herein, the publisher assumes no responsibility for any errors or omissions. No liability is assumed for damages that may result from the use of information contained within.

BlueRose Publishers takes no responsibility for any damages, losses, or liabilities that may arise from the use or misuse of the information, products, or services provided in this publication.

For permissions requests or inquiries regarding this publication, please contact:

BLUEROSE PUBLISHERS
www.BlueRoseONE.com
info@bluerosepublishers.com
+91 8882 898 898
+4407342408967

ISBN: 978-93-6261-143-7

Cover Design: Sadhna Kumari
Typesetting: Pooja Sharma

First Edition: July 2024

TO BELOVED ACHAN AND AMMA,
MY GUIDING LIGHTS, THANK YOU FOR ILLUMINATING MY PATH
WITH LOVE AND WISDOM.

Contents

1. Introduction 1
2. The Golden Era of Radios 8
3. Mango Talks 12
4. *Pulavaanibham*: A Village Fair of the People, For the People and By the People 16
5. Porter's Rest: Monuments of a Lost World. 20
6. Village Radio Kiosk of a Bygone Era. 23
7. Fountain Pen: The Magnificent Writing Machine. 26
8. The Gate 30
9. Amma and Her Goats 33
10. *Pothichoru:* The Taste of Tradition. 36
11. *Kettu Thengu*: The Pledging of Coconut Palm. 38
12. The Wandering Merchants of Kerala: A Forgotten Genre of Traders 41
13. Christmas In Kochi: Rose-Tinted Memories of a Colorful Period. 50
14. Vibrant Village Ponds 54
15. Requiem For a Grandma Tree 57
16. *Manappadam:* My First Encyclopaedia. 60
17. Village Vistas. 62
18. Ruminations on Sibling Relationship. 64
19. Ambujakshy: A Chef Extraordinaire and Her Culinary Excellence. 70

20. Parambikkulam: A Journey to Tranquility. 75

21. *Chayakkada*: Kochi's Village Tea Shops. 81

22. Match Makers of Yesteryears. 84

23. Free Ranging Village Dogs. 88

24. Amma and Her Reading Sessions 91

25. Minimalism as a Way of Village Life 94

26. Driven By Wheels: My Automotive Obsessions. 98

27. Kerala's Water Wells: A Source of Life and Culture. 102

28. The Mysterious Disappearance of M.V. Kairali: "The Titanic of Kerala". 105

29. Sanchayika: Piggy Banks to Passbooks; A History of Student Savings in Yesteryears. 108

30. The Revenge of Chandrabhanu and The Great Fire of Cochin. 111

31. The Village Library and the Fascinating World of Book 114

32. Malayalam: A Language in Transition. 118

33. Willingdon Island: An Oasis of Quietude 122

34. The Fascinating Story of Watches in India 127

35. Unni *Aasaan*: The Guiding Light on My Path of Knowledge. 131

36. *Pappadam*: The Quintessential Culinary Accompaniment 136

37. Classes Underneath the Banyan Trees. 140

38. Kerosene Lamps and Petromax in an Age of Darkness .. 144

39. *Vazhivilakkukal*: The Village Street Lights Through Decades 147

40. Kishore & Rahim: Echoes of Lost Innocence..................151

41. The Curious Life of Kochumariam 158

42. Prabhakaran and Thankappan: The Celebrated Village Musicians...162

43. *Chavittunaatakam:* The Exotic Dance-Drama of Kerala...165

44. *Kodathy Ammavan*: The Judge, Jury and Executioner of an Ancient Family...171

45. From Postmaster to Healer: Anchal Master's Remarkable Odyssey..174

46. Silent Valley: Expedition to a Precious Yet Vulnerable Evergreen Forest..179

47. On Greetings Cards 185

48. Monsoon Magic of Bygone Decades.....................................189

49. The Crazy World of Anthappan. 194

50. Amma and Her Culinary Excellence.....................................197

51. The Tale of a "Crime" and "the Punishment" 202

52. Fort Kochi: The Land where History, Culture, Traditions and Memories Coexist..205

53. *Chaya* And *Kadi*- A Nostalgic Journey Through Kerala's Evening Snacks. 212

54. Fathers' Day Thoughts. 215

55. A Village Beyond Caste and Class...219

56. Achan's Autumn Years: A Friendship Woven Through Time...223

57. On Photography in a Bygone Era 226

58. On the Art of Letter Writing..229

59. Ancient Houses of Kerala..232

60. Night of the Fireflies 236

61. Whispers of the Lost: The Silent Tale of our Vanishing Flora 239

62. The Hindu and Some Evergreen Memories 247

The Bookend 250

1. Introduction

In the sun-drenched summer afternoons in our front courtyard, I reveled in the warmth that enveloped me. The annual vacation days unfolded in the sprawling expanse of our homestead, where time seemed to stretch infinitely. But it was the moonlit nights that held magic. I would lie supine in Amma's lap, gazing at the star-studded sky, feeling the universe cradle me.

The evenings were equally enchanting. With his adventurous past, Achan spun tales that transported me to distant lands. My second brother, a master raconteur, with a penchant for exaggeration, regaled us with war stories—the lone battle fought and won. And the eldest brother, quick-witted and mischievous, peppered our conversations with wisecracks that left us laughing until our sides hurt.

Then came the first rain of the season—a symphony of droplets on tiled roofs. We'd rush outside, paper boats in hand, to set sail in rainwater rivulets. The old mango tree in our front courtyard stood sentinel, its expanding branches forming a gigantic canopy. Under its leafy shelter, I battled imaginary characters, my heart racing as I fought invisible foes.

And who could forget the make-believe horror stories? My sister, with her flair for the dramatic, narrated spine-chilling tales of ghosts and supernatural beasts that sent shivers down my spine. I'd huddle under the quilt, wide-eyed and breathless, half-terrified and wholly captivated.

Now, at sixty-three, I stand on the same land—the sacred ground where I spent all those childhood years. The memories cling to the soil, woven into the very fabric of this place. The sunsets paint the horizon in hues of nostalgia, and the mango tree still whispers secrets to the wind. It's a landscape etched not only in soil but also in the chambers of my heart.

My childhood friends were a motley crew, Obby, the handsomest and most intelligent in the bunch, Robert, the doubting Tom, Rahim, the most mature in the lot, Kishore, the innocent country lad, Gracy, the fragile and coy village girl, Naju the most obedient lass, Mumtaz, the charming girl, Henry the chubby, the village boys who take fiendish delight in hurting street dogs. Watcher, our loyal dog remained a mute witness and guarded our privacy. A childhood painted with hues of love and warmth. A life of innocence and adventure, teenage reveries, gruesome tragedies, what a whimsical and wonderful childhood I had!

This is where my story *Kerala Kaleidoscope* begins. I was born and raised in Palluruthy, a small, nondescript village in old Cochin, now referred to as West Kochi where I had a lively and clamorous childhood and early adulthood years in the large family along with my grandmother, father, mother, three sisters and two brothers. As my siblings got married, our family gradually grew with the arrival of three adorable brothers-in-law and two charming sisters-in-law. I was born in late 1961, as the sixth child of Thaiveettil Natarajan and Pullyadath Janaki Natarajan with two caring brothers and three affectionate sisters. Raised by an aging, disciplinarian father and an ailing but caring middle-aged mother in the company of five siblings as their youngest brother. Joys and challenges, pains and pleasures, childhood maladies – revisiting a splendidly marvelous formative year. When I was born my father was already a part of the Air Force, a job which took him to faraway locations every few years, when my eldest sister was married off, I was hardly two. I grew up in a sleepy village of rustic charm where culture and agriculture were inseparably intertwined. The village had a vast expanse of paddy fields, the frontiers of which were separated by mud bunds lined with coconut palms. Small canals crisscrossed the landscape which were used for irrigation and water transport. The village had plenty of green, splendid *Vellari paadam* where yellow cucumbers, snap melons (*pottu vellari*), bitter gourd, spinach, and other vegetables grew abundantly. Retting coconut husks, separating *chakiri*, the coir yarns from the retted husks, and later spinning them into coir were the main avocations of the men and women who belonged to the lower strata of the society. Back then my village was a spectacular place with lush green vegetation everywhere. We had no proper roads worth the name, only the dusty village alleys which meandered through the countryside lined with thickets where snakes dwelled at night in the darkness, no electricity was available in our vicinity, and our nights were lit up with kerosene lamps, so was piped drinking water, which we made good with water collected from numerous ponds and no automobiles except the hand-pulled cart for transporting materials and hand pulled rickshaw for transporting men. The main arterial road which cuts through the village was lined with numerous trees on either side which spread their branches forming a thick and continuous canopy through which shafts of sunlight filtered in. The nearest petrol stations were at Mattancherry halt where there used to be three fuel stations in close proximity owned by Burmah Shell, Caltex, and Essar. To commute, people depended heavily on water transport, which was provided by motorboats and *machuwa*, a kind of non-motorized wooden boats. Ending years of anxious wait, finally we got a telephone in the early nineties and the number was shared among our neighbors. At unearthly hours strangers phoned us requesting for their friends or relatives in our neighborhood on line to convey emergency messages much to the consternation of Achan. A radio kiosk in the village was a dependable source of news and entertainment. The main entertainment for the villagers was the Tamil and Malayalam cinemas which were exhibited at the nearby Jayalakshmi Talkies. For the latest releases, we had to go to Patel Talkies, once a landmark of old Kochi, at Thoppumpady, the nearest town. It was more than three miles away from where we lived and we took the tortuous route of the village path which passed through the middle of the paddy fields. The memory of watching *Chemmeen*, a classic film, which was the first South Indian movie to win the President's Gold Medal for Best Film, at Zina theatre at Fort Kochi is still fresh in my mind. In that Black and White era whenever there was an electricity failure during the show, which was quite common, we had to wait, sometimes for hours together, till the supply was resumed. Occasions were not rare when we had to come again to the theatre the next day with the old tickets to watch the remaining part of the show which was interrupted by the electricity failure. The villagers thoroughly enjoyed *Bharatanatyam, Mohiniyattam, Kathakali, Ottanthullal, Chakyarkooth,* and *Kathaaprasangam*, the one-man show of storytelling similar to the present-day stand-up comedy, which would be staged during temple festivals.

During hot mid-summer days, we would engage in tween-age mischiefs like catching *Kuzhiyana*, the antlions, from their cozy pits in loose soil along the periphery of the house and placing them in small pits covered with small glass pieces and watch them catching insects with gleeful choruses. We had a crazy childhood when we used to spend sleepless nights after secretly keeping fragments of *Mayilpeeli*, the peacock feather, deep inside the textbooks without exposing it to the sky in the foolish belief that it would give birth to new feathers. Though the feather delivery never happened, the futile exercise never disappointed us and it indeed was part of everyday ecstasies. In the bushes along the sides of the fence *Uppan*, the Crow Pheasants, lived happily and their cry in deep voice reverberated in the air which frightened me. *Kulakkozhi*, the white breasted Water Hens, lived peacefully in the bamboo patches near the family pond. The unexpected visit of *Pachakuthira*, the grasshopper, enthralled us as it was considered as the harbinger of wealth. The croaking of frogs, which was in fact the announcement of an impending rain, fascinated us. In the morning, we would be greeted by a kaleidoscope of colorful butterflies fluttering around in the garden, gleaming in the early morning sun shine.

Together we celebrated hilariously all major festivals like Onam, Vishu, Pooja, Bakri Eid, Ramzan, Christmas, and Easter, with religious fervor and extraordinary enthusiasm in a truly secular way. So were festivities related to the local temples, churches, and mosques. A vast majority of the villagers were from the marginalized sections of the population, and they lived in penury. Educated people were a tiny minority and they were keenly interested in reading, for which they visited the local libraries. But almost all of them had firm opinions about political issues. Village tea shops doubled as centers of discussions where they hotly debated political and social issues endlessly. Toddy shops were an integral component of village life where drunkards fought on trivial matters under alcoholic stupor. Barbar shops were frequented by youths not only for haircuts but also for reading newspapers and secretly gazing at the film magazines with colorful center spreads of scantily clad film stars and for a free exchange of gossip.

Health care system of our village was taken care of by the village medics of the class of Anchal Master and Raghavan *Vaidyar*, while apothecaries like Padmanabhan compounder and Gangadharan compounder crudely performed minor surgeries using their equally crude surgical methods. The villagers, however, had great faith in their surgical skills. Back then we had a couple of allopathy clinics where people thronged for treatments of serious ailments. Later, by the early seventies, an allopathy doctor, who was quite friendly and affable, came to the locality much to the relief of the people. His name was Dr.

Abubacker Koya, whose Riyaz Clinic functioned in a small two-room facility where people huddled. The clinic continued to function till early 2020 and when he died a few months later there were outpourings of touching recollections about the "people's doctor" which were posted on the social media. For medical emergencies people approached Government Maharaja's Hospital at Mattancherry.

Suddenly the India- Pak war had erupted casting its shadows over the village. It gave sleepless nights to Amma as she deeply and persistently worried about the safety and well-being of her two sons and husband who were on the war front. Then there was a talk about an imminent attack on Kochi by Pakistan which had shuddered us. The village was in the grip of an unknown fear. We were instructed to observe a complete black out at night in the event of a warning siren. Though the sirens were indeed sounded a few times to be followed by black out, nothing happened. And finally, to the relief of everyone, the war ended. Children in our school celebrated the occasion by taking out a victory procession through the streets around the school shouting slogans. The leaders in the front shouted slogans while the cheerful children enthusiastically repeated them in perfect harmony. I remember one such slogan was *"Yahya Khante vediyunda Bharathamakkalkku ariyunda"* which meant "the bombs of Yahya Khan are rice dumplings for the children of Bharat". (Agha Muhammed Yahya Khan was the then president of Pakistan). My elder brother Rajiv had won a special mention and a medal from the President of India for his meritorious service during the India-Pak war which brought laurels to the whole family and a hot topic for Amma which she proudly shared with her neighborhood women during their gossip sessions. And the event had given me unlimited bragging rights using which I shared the story with my classmates and friends, of course, lacing up with my fanciful additions.

My occasional visits to famed places in Kochi like Willingdon Island, Fort Kochi, and Mattancherry had always been pleasant experiences. Mattancherry bazar with its *paandika saala*, the godowns of enormous sizes, where spices, coir and other products were stored had always amazed me. I thoroughly enjoyed that brief but enchanting visits with unrestrained razzmatazz.

Sadly, in my once beautiful village, fireflies no longer glow, the family pond along with the Water Hens just vanished, and the bushes where the Crow Pheasants once nested disappeared. The *Pachakuthira*, which brought wealth and prosperity, no longer dances in our homes. The once-abundant *appuppanthaadi* and *manchadikkuru* have also disappeared. The presence of butterflies has been reduced to a few. All those amazing village spectacles have vanished during the evolutionary process of our landscape.

My life has been molded by a series of fortuitous combinations of circumstances and fate. Like many of my generation, I have the felicity of living in two millennia and two different centuries as I have lived the best and most eventful years of my life in the 20th century and still enjoying the worldly blessings of the 21st century, a rare privilege indeed. In hindsight, I feel as if I lived two lives in two entirely different worlds in a single birth.

This book is an honest recollection of events, people, and places which I had witnessed during the transmogrification of old Cochin into a modern and vibrant city called Kochi, with historical facts where they are needed to reinforce the narrative. A sepia-tinted view of adolescent life, jasmine scented recollection of childhood memories and a few heartbreaking stories too which life has presented with. With these words, I invite you to walk alongside me as I trace the bygone years. A mélange of memories.

2. The Golden Era of Radios

Radio had reached our sleepy village in old Kochi only by the early sixties when a few influential families in the locality brought foreign Radio sets. Then it was thrilling news among the villagers, and it was widely rumored that those sets were surreptitiously brought from Persia, present-day Iran.

Way back in the late nineteen sixties, my father brought a new transistor radio during one of his annual leaves from the Indian Air Force. It was a medium-sized transistor radio which was encased in an elegant leather case. The case had several windows exposing various switches and a long band display. On the black-colored glass display, it was written in small white letters MW and SW, abbreviations for Medium Wave and Short Wave with frequencies in minute letters. At the bottom of the leather case, it was written in golden letters "National 2 speaker Deluxe". In those days the popular radio brands were Philips and Murphy and brands like Panasonic, Sanyo, National, and Sharp appeared in the village only many years later. A few hotels and tea shops of the small town had mammoth-size valve radios that blared high-decibel film songs being aired by Vividh Bharati and Radio Ceylon. FM stations became a reality only by the early nineties. There were a couple of radio repairers in the locality who enjoyed considerable respect.

The most popular among the programs was the serialized play aired every Sunday night, and film songs. We excitedly waited for the occasional airing of sound track of block buster films, *sabdarekha*, which enlivened our evenings. People thoroughly enjoyed *Kandathum Kettathum*, the skit which was a social satire based on contemporary realities in society. We eagerly looked forward to the many cultural programs broadcasted during Onam. In those days the running commentary of Nehru Trophy Boat Race of Alappuzha enthralled the listeners. Commentary presented a word picture with graphic details of the race which was more enjoyable than viewing the race itself. Eminent commentators like Nagavally R S Kurup fascinated the audience with their inimitable verbosity. So was the running commentary of the Santosh Trophy Football Tournament. *Praadesika Vaarthakal*, the local news read by Pratapan and *Kautuka Vaarthakal*, the fascinating news in Ramachandran's characteristic, inimitable style of presentation was a different experience. Equally captivating were the news reading by Rani in her melodious voice and Sankara Narayanan in his deep resonating voice from Delhi. Achan made it his habit to listen to the 9 O'clock English news bulletin which I could barely understand. When the national emergency was declared on 25th June,1975, the news was broken by AIR in its night bulletin. Achan and two brothers seemed shocked by the news as they could be seen engaged in serious discussion till late into the night which was unusual. I could not understand the reason for their anxious debates. Later, Rajiv Chettan explained to me the political fallout of the emergency. I could not comprehend all those arcane details.

Sometime in the late sixties, my uncle Narayanan from Bombay brought to Amma's ancestral home an automatic radio-cum record player of Philips. The record player had been equipped with a turntable in which 10 record plates could be stacked one above the other on a lever. Once a record is completed playing, the tonearm of the player would automatically pull down the next plate and play automatically. (I remember in those days most gramophone records were from the famed HMV brand with its iconic logo of Nipper, the dog, staring at a phonograph listening to His Master's Voice. It was produced by The Gramophone Company of the US, a company which enjoyed international renown). The arrival of a sophisticated record player had created a sensation in the neighborhood and became a talking point of the village. When I reached along with Amma the house was crowded with curious onlookers from neighboring houses who were excitedly waiting to see the functioning of the magical instrument. I watched in disbelief the way the player automatically selected the records one by one from a bunch of ten and played one after other. For the villagers it was an incredible equipment because they were used to the conventional ones where one must replace the record after playing the earlier one. The next day in school I bragged about uncle's new record player in a highly exaggerated manner but many of my friends were skeptical about my fanciful narrative and a few among them even questioned the veracity of my story.

In the late sixties, only two independent Malayalam stations were available, Trivandrum and Calicut, while Alleppey was just a relay station of Trivandrum. The signal strength of Calicut station was quite feeble and marred by disturbances. These stations were in the Medium Wave. In the shortwave, the favorite stations were Vividh Bharati and the Malayalam transmission from Sri Lanka Broadcasting Corporation.

By the mid-seventies, transistor radios had become a common household equipment and one could walk along the roads and alleys enjoying uninterrupted music because it flowed from every house that lined up the streets without breaking continuity. In those uneventful days, people turned to radio programs to alleviate boredom. The eighties witnessed spectacular changes in radio technology and the arrival of two-in-one radio with a cassette player revolutionized the way we enjoyed radio.

In the early days of radio in India, owning and operating a radio set required a license. In the 1970s, this license cost a modest Rs. 15 per year, which Achan diligently paid at the nearby Palluruthy Post Office. However, this requirement was later discontinued.

Despite the arrival of TV, all these years the importance of radio as a mass communication and entertainment medium has not waned. As a routine, once I start my car quite impulsively my hands reach out to the car stereo to switch it on. In a sense I'm "radioactive".

Like reading, radios fire our fertile imagination in umpteen ways. Mercedes McCambridge, American actress, once famously remarked, *"Radio is truly the theatre of the mind. The listener constructs the sets, colors them from his own palette, and sculpts and costumes the characters who perform in them".*

3. Mango Talks

Mango trees are ubiquitous fruit-bearing tropical trees of India. A wide variety of mangos with shapes, sizes, and tastes as diverse as their names are available.

Mangoes are quintessential in Kerala, found everywhere from highways and village alleys to open grounds, private groves, school yards, church and temple courtyards, and house yards—in short, in every available vacant space. As it is a robust plant with great survival instincts it can withstand the hot and humid summers and cold and watery monsoons with equal strength.

Kerala is home to a plethora of diverse varieties of mangoes including native varieties such as *Chandrakkaran, Moovandan, Kalluketty, Neelam, Nettu Kuzhiyan, Naattumaavu, Chakkarakutty, Kappa manga*, and the golden colored *Suvarna Rekha. Thenmaavu*, the honey mango tree has been immortalized in literature by Vaikom Muhammed Basheer, the Sultan of storytelling, in his celebrated short story by the same name.

Apart from the home-grown species, a multitude of non-native species are abundantly available in Kerala including species like *Alphonso, Sindhura, Banganapalle, Malgoa, Priyur, Raspuri, Kalapady, Gomanga* and *Kilichundan* (totapuri) which acquired the name from its shape which resembles the lip of a parrot.

In bygone decades every Kerala household had at least one mango tree in the courtyard. In our front courtyard, there was a huge *Moovandan* mango tree with its vast canopy shading the courtyard through which beams of sunlight filtered forming irregular shaped shades on the ground. We still have fond memories of this mango tree, which was over sixty years old when it suddenly fell one stormy night during torrential rain. Every year Amma would engage a mango plucker during the mango season by mid-summer who would come with a *"kolli"*, a long wooden pole fitted with a sickle and a small bag at one end, to pluck the fruits. The fruits thus plucked would be collected in the bag. Fallen fruits were not used for ripening and would be used raw in curries. The plucked mangoes would be collected in a few large bamboo baskets and Amma would distribute a few pieces to every house in the neighborhood. Our share would be kept for ripening in large copper vessels (*chembu*) lined with alternate layers of hay and mango. The remaining fruits would be kept under the cots for ripening over a bed of hay which would be covered with another layer of hay. As the fruits began to ripen, the whole house would be filled with the sweet smell of mangoes. It was the task of Achan that every morning he would peel and cut to slice half a dozen mangoes which would be the accompaniment of rice *Puttu* for breakfast. Using raw mango Amma used to prepare *chammanthy* by grinding it with scraped coconut, green chili and a bit of salt on a grinding stone. After finishing her job, she would mix a handful of rice with the leftover *chammanthy* which adhered to the grinding stone and would put the rice balls into my mouth. I find my vocabulary woefully inadequate to describe the mouthwatering taste of the mixture which I relished to my heart's content. My grandmother and Amma used to make a very special Mango seed *Appam* by mixing the paste made from the mango seed kernel with rice flour, coconut and jagerry. Mango seed *Appam* is believed to contain various bioactive compounds that possess a range of medicinal properties, including antioxidant, anti-inflammatory, antimicrobial, anticancer, anti-diabetic, cardiovascular, and immune-enhancing activities. These compounds make Mango seed Appam a potential natural remedy for various health conditions.

During our childhood days it was our favorite pastime to hurl stones at the mango trees in full bloom in the neighbor's yard. The elderly woman of the house would scold us and once asked me to hurl stones at my own mango trees rather than targeting hers. The news soon reached Amma's ears, and I had to face the consequences in the evening.

At one time, we had as many as 24 fully-grown mango trees of different varieties in our courtyard. A true mango aficionado, Achan would bring seeds of rare varieties from different places and plant them in our courtyard.

During our childhood days, my siblings and I used to brush our teeth with mango leaves. After removing the midrib, we would curl them up and rub them with *umikkari*, the burnt and powdered rice husk. *Ammumma* (maternal grandmother) used to tell us that mango leaves contain certain medicinal products which would protect our teeth against cavitation and tooth aches.

Mango is a customary culinary ingredient in Kerala which found its use in unique preparations like *mambazha pulisserry, kadu manga*, mango cured in salt, which is used for *uppumanga* chutney, mango *chammanthy*, mango pickle, and also as a universal ingredient in many kinds of vegetarian and non-vegetarian preparations. Ripe mangoes are used to prepare squash, jam, purée, and juices. In short, mangoes are inseparably linked to the culinary and cultural ethos of Kerala. Every year July 22 is celebrated as "National Mango Day" in adoration of this highly nutritious, sweet, and delicious fruit known by the appellatory sobriquet "King of Fruits". Interestingly, *"mangatholi samsaram"* is a commonly used idiom of colloquial tone in Malayalam which means nonsensical, often ridiculous talks. It loosely translates as "mango peel talks" in English.

Modern science reveals that mango peel is rich in antioxidants and fiber, offering numerous health benefits. We can no longer dismiss its value. Let's hope this isn't just idle talk about mango peels.

4. *Pulavaanibham*: A Village Fair of the People, For the People and By the People

"The land of legends and lores" is an epithet frequently used to describe Kerala which reflects its cultural legacy and tradition. There had been many rituals and religious practices prevalent in the past centuries which were unique to Kerala. *Pulavaanibham* is one such unique festival of the downtrodden and marginalized section of the people who had been the victims of exploitation by feudal chieftains and aristocratic landlords for generations.

Pulavaanibham, which means the trade fair of the *Pulayas*, is a quintessential regional trade fair that in contemporary society is truly rural set against an urban background. *Pulaya* is a scheduled caste community of Kerala, who made a livelihood by toiling in farmlands and making handcrafted traditional household items and are amongst the most downtrodden of the marginalized population. They were treated as untouchables by the upper castes and in the olden days, they were not allowed to enter temples owned by the forward communities.

Azhakiyakavu Bhagavathy Temple of Palluruthy is one such temple where untouchability was practiced till a few decades ago. It is an ancient 500-year-old temple and famed as a major temple in the erstwhile Kingdom of Kochi. The presiding deity, Bhagavathy, was deeply worshipped and greatly trusted by the local populace. She was considered the *Desa Devatha*, meaning the "Goddess of the Land". In the days of yore the whole West Kochi was ravaged by smallpox and many people perished. It was believed that the epidemic was the manifestation of the wrath of Bhagavathy. The solution was to appease the village Goddess which was promptly performed by believers of the upper castes. Being untouchables, *Pulayas* and similar castes in the lower rungs of the caste hierarchy could not offer worship. They appealed to the Maharaja of Kochi for permission to enter the temple and to perform poojas to appease Bhagavathy and escape her wrath. The King of Kochi was benevolent and sympathetic indeed and allowed these subaltern people to visit the temple, have *darshan*, and fulfill their votive *(nercha)* in the temple once a year. For this, they were allowed to enter the temple through the rarely used northern gate instead of the main gate on the eastern side. This day falls on the last Thursday of the Malayalam month *Dhanu*, which is usually the second week of January.

In the olden days, the *Pulaya* and other communities belonging to the scheduled castes and tribes would throng the temple on this auspicious day to offer prayers. As the sun set, they would arrive in the evening, bathed in its warm afterglow, carrying a brass plate called *thaalam*. The plate was adorned with raw rice, colorful fruits, fragrant flowers, and a half-cut coconut containing a lighted oil lamp. The procession was accompanied by the vibrant rhythms of *chenda melam*, an ensemble of drummers. They would perambulate along the highway and would enter the temple through the side gate to offer their prayers. In the distant past, on the occasion, they used to bring with them an array of their agricultural products like yam(*chena*), coco yam (*chembu*), tapioca, sweet potato, sugarcane, and the like. People also brought with them homemade agricultural implements such as spade (*manvetty*), shovel, knives of varying size and shape, grinding stone (*arakallu*), hand crafted, braided mat made of screw pine leaf (*thazha paya*), hand-held fans of screw pine leaf (*visary*), bamboo baskets of different shape and sizes (*kutta*), winnow (*muram*), coconut scraper fitted on a wooden platform (*chirava*), mortar and pestle made of granite (*ural* and *ulakka*), earthen pottery ware like pan (*chatty*), pot (*kalam*), braided bamboo mat (*panambu*), and a lot more. Gradually, the village fair evolved into a mega rural fair where people would put up temporary, makeshift stalls all along the sides of the thoroughfare and in the sprawling temple maidan. Quite interestingly, the best part of the sales happened after nightfall, especially after mid night though in those days, night life was something unimaginable. The fair famed itself for rare items like dry shrimp and fish, and salted shark meat which were conspicuous by their absence in other similar fairs. There would be many dedicated stalls exclusively for these items.

The most remarkable aspect of *Pulavaanibham* is its self-organizing nature, where it comes together seamlessly every year without the need for any formal organizers, making it a true people's fair in every sense. In our childhood days, we waited with eagerness for this once-a-year event where Amma used to purchase plastic toys, dates, rice flakes, puffed rice, sweet meats of varying colors, sugar cane stem, *murukku*, and *Bombay mittayi* (cotton candy) for us.

In recent times, while the fair still exudes the same enthusiasm and joy, the essence of *Pulavaanibham* as a traditional village fair has gradually given way to a more urbanized fair, characterized by the proliferation of Chinese-made goods, reminiscent of any other commercial fair. In other words, *Pulavaanibham* has lost much of its village flavor and sheen once touted as the largest rural trade fair of its kind in the state.

A couple of weeks ahead of the festivities the traders would descend from faraway places and their shanties would be lined up alongside the main roads.

In modern times, as a sequel to the historic Temple Entry Proclamation in 1936, which allows people of all castes, including traditionally marginalized castes to enter temples, the *Pula Nercha* has lost its religious significance. Today it remains as the grim reminder of the dark era in the history of Kerala where one's caste and creed mattered more than anything else and played dominant roles in shaping one's destiny. Nevertheless, *Pulavaanibham* is to stay here as a secular urban festival of the people, by the people, and for the people.

5. Porter's Rest: Monuments of a Lost World

Athaani, Porter's rest has a fascinating history in Kerala. Several decades ago, such porter's rest had been erected in every nook and corner of the state by erstwhile rulers of the princely states of Malabar, Kochi, and Travancore. Feudal landlords of yore and many temples had also erected such porters' rest in their respective localities. It symbolizes more than physical rest; it embodies the hardships and struggles of a generation of working-class people who labored hard to eke out a living and their indomitable spirit.

In the past, there were no proper roads, only narrow, winding village paths and narrow alleys that connected the villages. People used these routes to transport goods and materials. Along the busy trade routes and adjacent to markets, one could see porter's rests, where laborers would take a break from their strenuous work.

A porter's rest is comprised of two heavy stone pillars erected side by side a few feet apart, atop which a third flat slab of similar size and shape is placed forming a gigantic bench. They usually stood five to six feet above ground. They had been erected with the noble intention of easing the burden of porters and traveling salesmen carrying heavy loads. This kind of arrangement immensely helped tired porters carrying heavy loads on their heads to unload them comfortably onto the porters' rest and relax for a while. When they resumed their journey after relaxing and calming down themselves, they could easily put the heavy load single-handedly on their head. They were in fact "take-a-break" facilities available to the public in the olden days.

They are indeed monuments of a bygone era. They had a resemblance to Stonehenge of an ancient time.

In bygone decades, these stone structures were erected by the rulers of erstwhile princely states of Malabar, Kochi, and Travancore and by feudal landlords and affluent aristocratic people as monuments to honor some members of the ruling elite. Many porters rest had inscriptions on them in old Malayalam or Tamil.

They seldom stand in isolation. In most cases, the porters' rest would be in the immediate vicinity of a well full of clean drinking water which served to quench the thirst of the exhausted porters. In some places, the porters' rest would be associated with a small but comfortable hut with a huge cauldron-like stone structure carved in granite called *karinkal thotty* filled with drinking water or *"sambharam"*, the butter milk sprinkled with sliced green chili, ginger, curry leaves and salt. Together, they formed part of the village landscape. The hut along with the huge basin containing water is called *Thanneer Pandhal* or water sheds. *Vazhiyambalam* is a slightly refined version, having more space which provided a safe resting place to travelers of the olden days. Back then, this was a great solace for long-distance travelers and traders. A number of such porter's rest were found in many places around Kochi until a few decades ago. Near the village office in my hometown of Palluruthy in Kochi, a porter's rest still stands intact despite the several developments that have taken place in its vicinity.

Almost all such *Chumaduthangi* and *Thanner Pandhal* were wantonly destroyed for the sake of development. These ancient artifacts of historical importance are indeed the relics of a bygone era and need to be protected. Next time we pass by a porter's rest, let us salute those who labored silently- the porters, carriers and the unsung heroes who played a role in shaping the history of Kerala.

6. Village Radio Kiosk of a Bygone Era

In the heart of Palluruthy once stood a modest community radio kiosk. Operated by the Block Panchayat, this quaint unassuming hexagonal concrete structure was located near the then National Extension Service (NES) Block Office, alongside the national highway. The building had large, glass-paned windows on all sides which allowed sunlight to filter, with an elegantly manicured lawn in front of it. Today the village office occupies the very same spot where this "radio station" once existed. There was not much gadgetry, no digital devices in the building. Instead, there was a large valve regenerative radio encased in a sturdy wooden cabinet with a 'magic eye,' emitting a mystical green glow. It had an amplifier and a small cone-shaped grey horn speaker, turned north to ensure that people gathered in the vast ground could hear clearly. Atop the kiosk, an elongated wire gauze stretched between two poles served as the aerial, capturing signals from near and far. It was as vital as the radio itself.

The functioning of the radio kiosk was limited only to a couple of hours in the evening preluding nightfall. The operation of the radio was a prerogative of Narayanan, a tall, fair complexioned man who was the employee of the Panchayat. He was tasked with collecting taxes from the property owners for which he visited households. In those days, it was indeed an unenviable job to collect taxes as many defaulted payment and Narayanan had to visit several times to collect the taxes from a reluctant citizenry. After his regular job of tax collection during the daytime, he moonlighted as the custodian cum operator of the public radio kiosk. Occasions were not rare when he would be in an inebriated state, oblivious of the world around him.

He would come by 5 in the evening, open the large wooden door of the kiosk with a bang, and start tuning the stations. By this time several people including youths and village elders from the locality would have gathered in the sprawling village *maidan*. We, the children, had always aspired to have an inside view of the radio room which Narayanan vehemently and consistently denied much to our dismay.

Back then, we had only two independent Medium Wave (MW) radio stations in Kerala namely Thiruvananthapuram and Kozhikode. Thrissur station was a relay station of Thiruvananthapuram, while Alappuzha station was yet to be commissioned. Narayanan had tuned only to Thiruvananthapuram, as Kozhikode station had low radio signal strength and hence, difficult to get tuned and constant disturbances marred the quality of the broadcast.

When Narayanan switched on the radio and tuned the station every evening, the listeners were greeted initially with only a whistling sound. This would continue for a while, to be followed by the famed signature tune of Akashvani. (The hilarious part of the signature tune of AIR is that it is the creative work of Walter Kaufmann, a Jewish refugee and Director of Akashvani in 1937 who tuned this ubiquitous piece in Sivaranjani raga. For decades, this has been the wake-up music of millions of Indians). Regular programs like *Pradesika Varthakal* (regional newscast), *Vayalum Veedum* (farm and home), *Kambola nilavaram* ((Market update), and *Kaalaavastha* (weather forecast) would be followed by film songs from 7 to 7.25. From 7.25 to 7.35 there would be national news in Malayalam being relayed from AIR Delhi. We used to spend our evenings listening to the film songs which often mingled with the songs from the nearby Jayalakshmi Talkies. By this time, the night would have enveloped the whole village in a thick blanket of darkness. Electric streetlights were a rare luxury that only very few places were blessed with. After listening to the news headlines people would start their return homeward journey. After the Delhi news, Narayanan would switch off the radio and leave the kiosk marking the end of yet another hectic day in his life. Whether rain or shine, he continued his routine and he played an important role in disseminating information and enlightening a village about the major happenings in the world and also entertaining them with melodious film songs. In an era, when information technology was yet to take shape, Narayanan and his radio kiosk provided a window through which the villagers glimpsed the world, and came to know about many events of importance. It was through this radio that the villagers listened to news of the man landing on the moon which surprised them, while the news about Naxalite violence by the fire-breathing revolutionaries in Malabar frightened them to the core, whereas the news of the sudden death of Nehru shocked and saddened them profoundly.

When radio became commonplace, the public radio kiosk lost its importance and gradually the kiosk and its sole service provider Narayanan fell into oblivion. He was one among the numerous unsung heroes of our village.

7. Fountain Pen: The Magnificent Writing Machine

A person's handwriting is as unique as his fingerprint. The past two decades have witnessed revolutionary changes in the way we write. Writing the conventional way using tools like pen and pencil has increasingly been replaced by electronic gadgets like computers and smartphones. Today's youth and new generation students are reluctant to write with a pen or a pencil. Rather they prefer to scribble in their note pads. I fear if this trend continues, in the not-too-distant future, we will have a generation who will be incapable of writing by hand. The art and skill of penmanship would be alien to them. The over-dependence on electronic devices has already seriously impacted their ability to write.

Even when students are compelled to write their notes and assignments, they use shoddy, inexpensive, single-use plastic pens. Such pens, after use, are carelessly discarded, posing severe environmental problems. Students and youths should be encouraged to use fountain pens which one can use for many years, instead of ballpoint or gel pens with limited life span.

I have a lifelong fascination and deep passion for fountain pens. Realizing my affection, recently for my birthday my son and daughter gifted me two precious pens, son an expensive Sheaffer pen and daughter an equally expensive Parker fountain pen using which I am penning this piece.

In our school, till 4th standard only pencils were allowed but when prompted to 5th, to our sheer joy we were allowed to use ink pen. Back then students were not permitted to write board examinations using ball point pens. However, rules were changed in the early eighties, which allowed students to use ball point pens to write examinations.

At UP school our science teacher had gold topped, blue colored Hero pen which he displayed proudly in his pocket. It had a pointed tip with a golden arrow and a small nib which imparted an enchanting look to the pen. I used to watch him write in small, round letters in his book with interest. I strongly desired to own a similar Hero pen which once I told my mother.

A few days later she bought a blue-colored fountain pen for me along with a bottle of Bril ink. "Chacha" was its brand which I instantly liked. In hindsight, I still feel the pleasure of writing with that pen in the glossy pages of Wisdom brand notebooks.

One day my friend told me that the color of a pen could be changed by treating it with turmeric powder. As suggested by him, I smeared my pen with turmeric paste for a few minutes and then it was completely wiped off. My friend was right indeed, the color did change; mine from an attractive Navy blue to a drab Green. This unexpected color change of my pen pained me. Though I washed it umpteen times, it failed to restore the original color. I cursed my friend for his ill advice while Amma scolded me for my misadventure.

In the olden days a fountain pen was a prized possession that lasted a lifetime. In old families when a patriarch died, his fountain pen and spectacles were used to be preserved as immortal memorabilia.

Near our school, there was a small shack where pens were repaired and if needed, he conducted an "organ transplant" like replacing the barrel, nib, or feed. Occasionally we used to clean our pen by dismantling it into individual parts, cleaning it with lukewarm water, wiping and then reassembling the various pieces. This kind of wellness treatment prolonged the life and quality of pens. They are durable and environment-friendly instruments.

I am deeply attached to my pens and treat them with great respect. It's the magical machine that transforms my thoughts into meaningful words and sentences. In our childhood days, we were taught to treat books and pens with respect and reverence, a custom we inherited from our forefathers.

My father had a profound passion for fountain pens. His enthusiasm was reignited when my cousin Rajan Mavunkal from Bombay gifted him a stunning black Hero pen, adorned with tiny stars in blue and golden yellow. Achan cherished this pen for a few days before passing it on to me, and I used it for several years. With this trusty pen, I wrote my BSc and MSc examinations, achieving high marks. I attribute a portion of my success to the auspicious pen. When my niece heard the story, she eagerly requested the pen, and I gifted it to her, albeit with some reluctance. However, she didn't quite match my academic achievements, thereby debunking the myth surrounding the pen's supposed luck

An ink pen has always been my constant companion. Way back in 1985, I joined an exporting company in Goa (my first job in a long series) where I had a brief and unsuccessful stint. To join for my debut job, Achan booked an air ticket and I went by Indian Airlines Kochi- Goa flight. As usual, I had my ink pen which I clipped on my pocket. Midway through, air hostesses came and pointed to my pocket which was by then completely drenched in black ink which leaked out through the pen. I learnt a lesson and in all my subsequent travel by air, I ensured that the ink from my pen was completely drained out.

International Fountainpen Day is observed on the first Friday in November every year. The day is observed by pen aficionados to promote the use of fountain pen and the enjoyment of writing in general.

SLICE OF HISTORY.

Obeying the request of Nehru, it was Prem Behari Narayan Raizada, who hand wrote the original of the voluminous Indian Constitution. He completed the task in six months with a fountain pen using 254 pen holder nibs of No: 303 in beautiful italic calligraphy. Till this day it remains as the longest hand written constitution. For this impressive task, he did not accept any remuneration from government, he instead insisted to write his name underneath each page of the mammoth manuscript; and on the last page his grandfather's name too alongside him. Nehru agreed, unhesitatingly.

During the independence struggle as part of making swadeshi products Mahatma Gandhi advised K.V. Ratnam in 1921 to make a pen of our own. He made one after a careful study of an imported fountain pen and had sent it to Gandhiji for his approval. Gandhiji liked the pen and commented that it was a good substitute for foreign pens. This heralded the beginning of Ratnam Pen Works.

TAIL PIECE.

As a tradition, after signing a death warrant, the judge, in a symbolic gesture, breaks the nib of the pen, which is not a law. This custom, which we follow even in present day, is a legacy we inherited from our erstwhile colonial masters.

"My two fingers on a typewriter have never connected with my brain. My hand on a pen does. A fountain pen, of course. Ball point pens are only good for filling out forms on a plane".

GRAHAM GREENE.

8. The Gate

It's a law of nature that the old and obsolete should give way to new ones.

A couple of years back, on a fine sunny day, the main gate in the front of my ancestral home was brought down to make way for building a new compound wall. In the morning, when I left for the office, it was there. But by the time I came back in the evening it had been reduced to a mangled mass of metal which was carelessly discarded in a corner of the courtyard. This indeed is a prelude to the construction of a new house for my nephew in his share of the land which he inherited from his mother. This has become an imperative as when my parents divided the family property amongst their six children through a will executed in late nineties, the front courtyard along with a large pond in the *kannimoola* was inherited by my elder sister Sheela. Interestingly, all of us except Sheela got prime plots adjoining the new main road with direct access to road.

Though the demolition of the old, rusted gate was inevitable, it brought a flurry of nostalgic memories to my mind.

Originally, we had a plot measuring 60 cents which Achan procured way back in the late sixties as two separate plots. The initial plot measuring 31 cents was acquired in late sixties from

Puthanpurackal family, an old Christian family. Subsequently, an adjoining piece of land measuring 29 cents was added to it later from Pothampilly family, another affluent family of the village.

Till the late seventies, the entire compound was fenced using thatched coconut leaves. The fence had to be mended and replaced, an annual exercise, which imposed a huge financial burden on our finances. Amma performed this task with recurring regularity. Achan at the far end of the seventies decided to construct a permanent brick wall skirting the whole property. Constructing a brick wall all around the perimeter of a 60-cent plot was then considered an uphill task which he completed in a phased manner. It was at this juncture Cochin Corporation approached him for land acquisition for the construction of the present New Forty-Foot Road which cut through our property on the western side. On the northern plot, a family lived as our tenants. Under the Land Reforms Rule, we were legally obliged to give 3.3 cents to the family, but Achan willingly donated 10 cents to the family. After the land acquisition for the road and his benevolent act of sacrificing 10 cents for the tenants, we were left with 32 cents around which the wall was constructed.

Achan had aspired that there should be an iron gate with an ornate design in the front. In those days, gates were very rare, and most village courtyards were open. A nearby welding workshop was tasked with the construction of the iron gate. The workshop owner came with a catalog containing myriad designs in every imaginable form. Achan consulted my elder sister and me to select a few designs of our liking. We meekly selected a couple of them from which he selected one to our surprise because, in such matters he seldom consulted us.

A few days later, the gate was brought home painted with a coat of red primer. The next evening when I came back from school the gate was already fixed in place, supported by a couple of bamboo poles. The work was done perfectly by Augustin, the head village mason assisted by his protege Xavier. From his expression, I understood that a beaming Achan was silently enjoying the elegance of the gate. Atop the two-piece gate the words NATARAJ BHAVAN were welded neatly in capital letters. A few days later Kochappan, (whom people mockingly referred to as Belt as he always wore trousers with suspenders even in his adulthood years) the village painter was hired and he neatly painted the gate and two massive pillars in a combination of black, white and grey which imparted unmatched beauty to the gate.

After I inherited the *tharavad*, a generous amount of money was spent on it to give a vast face lift, and the facade was changed westward facing the new road. Since then, the old gate was closed permanently and it fell into disuse exposing it to the vagaries of the climate. The demolition of the old gate prompted me to reminisce about the fond memories and the people associated with it, many of whom have since passed on. The occasion stirred up bittersweet nostalgia, recalling the joy and laughter we shared, now tinged with the melancholy of their absence.

"Each of us guard a gate of change that can only be opened from the inside."

Stephen Covey.

9. Amma and Her Goats

During my childhood years, it was Amma who shouldered the heavy burden of managing the family as Achan was posted in faraway locations of Indian Air Force camps. Amma displayed unparalleled prowess in household management with the paltry amount that Achan used to send every month. Knowing that the amount he sent every month was hardly sufficient to manage a family of six children, she engaged herself in small-time activities like goat rearing, chicken rearing and firewood trading. In this way, she garnered some additional income to supplement the monthly income. My eldest brothers and sisters used to help her wholeheartedly in her ventures. They would bring fresh cut grass and jackfruit leaves from the nearby market every evening as fodder for goats and brought coconut oil cake and groundnut oil cakes which Amma would dissolve in concentrated rice water and give to the goats. As far as I can remember, there were a couple of goats with their calves which were housed in a small, thatched shed beside the kitchen. She would tend them with extreme care and during the daytime she would take them out to the open courtyard tethered to long ropes where they would be allowed to forage freely on the grass and weeds which they savored heartily. In the early morning and evening, it was the responsibility of Amma to milk the goats and the milk would be collected in a brass vessel. After taking a small quantity for our use the rest would be sold to customers in the neighborhood. Amma used to give sweet names to her goats. Mani Kutty was her favorite.

As the mating time approached the nanny goat would start crying unusually, mostly on full moon nights announcing that she was in heat and ready for mating. In a day or two, Amma would take her to the neighborhood house where mature male goats (called Billy goats) were reared and leave her in his company. For the courtship to happen, the nanny would be tied close by Billy. After a few minutes, they would start making love to each other which would lead to the final act of copulation in an hour or so. The whole exercise would be over in a couple of hours and thereafter Amma would bring her back and tether her in the shed. The gestation period lasts for around 5 months. During this period, Amma would treat her with utmost care. It was Amma who did the role of a midwife and assisted the goat in delivery in a way a veterinarian could do. Normally, there would be two to three kids or sometimes even more. In those days, though we had a government veterinary hospital it was not of much help in such emergencies. The goat would cry loudly, unable to bear the excruciating pain of labor. As I was curious to know about the ways of a goat delivery, I would peep through the open window which Amma discouraged with a stern warning, and I obeyed her warning unquestionably.

When a milch goat ceases to yield milk after two or three deliveries, the usual practice was to sell the mother goat after retaining the kids. A tall, lanky, middle-aged Muslim man, dressed in a *kallimundu* and white banyan, would occasionally visit to buy goats, specifically looking for dry ones that would invariably be butchered for meat

While negotiating such goat deals, Amma always appeared tense. The trader, after fixing the deal, would give her a small sum as an advance and would promise to come on a later date with the balance amount to take the goat. On the day of the final deal, Amma would bathe the animal in the morning for one last time and would be served a sumptuous meal of grass, jackfruit leaves and a lavish porridge of rice water and oil cake. The day would be marked by an air of unusual calm and soulful silence as the animal that was part of our life for long years would soon be bidding farewell to us. The very thought would be an unsettling experience.

And finally, at the appointed time, the trader would come with the balance of money. After collecting the money, Amma would withdraw to the interior room asking the trader to untie the leash and take possession of the goat, instead of her handing over the animal to him directly as is the usual practice. It indeed was a highly emotional moment for all of us as the stranger forcibly took her away out of our courtyard amidst her cry of protestation. The most moving moment is when the animal would look back again and again and eyed us helplessly as she reluctantly followed the trader. It was to avoid the touching gaze of the innocent animal which she cared for and tended like a little child, that Amma retreated to the interior of the house while we watched helplessly as she bade final farewell to us. *ammee, ammee....* The goat's plaintive bleats were just heart-wrenching and would continue to haunt us for many more days. I felt a lump in my throat.

10. *Pothichoru:* The Taste of Tradition

Pothichoru in Malayalam means "packed rice meal". Such *Pothichoru* has been a symbol of a cultural legacy and in bygone decades it epitomized the typical South Indian culinary tradition and a way of life full of rustic charm. During my school days in Kochi, I was among the fortunate few to own a stainless-steel tiffin box which I used to carry in my school bag along with books. But most of my classmates used to bring their lunch neatly packed in plantain leaves over wrapped in newspapers.

It was in a fascinating way the food was packed in banana leaves. Back then everyone had a few plantains in their backyard and hence there was no dearth of banana leaves. For packing meals, tender leaves were the preferred choice. Larger leaves would be separated into two halves along the midrib. The freshly cut tender banana leaves were then gently heated over a hearth on a low flame. The purpose of this thermal conditioning was to make the leaf flexible so that it would not tear apart while being folded. Apart from making the leaf flexible, heating had also imparted a tantalizing aromatic fragrance which enriched the taste of the food it wrapped. At first, a few spoonfuls of hot rice would be spread into the leaf, then accompaniments like curry, pickles, and gravy would be poured over the rice. Usually, curries are buttermilk, *sambar*, or *rasam*. Special items like fish fry, and omelet would be packed separately in another piece of leaf and would be kept atop the other items. Thereafter, the entire bunch would be neatly packed in the plantain leaf and final wrapping with a newspaper piece. Students of those days would keep this food pack above their neatly stacked books and then the whole thing would be tied together with a rubber band. Packing food in plantain leaf was an art in itself and Amma was quite skillful in the art. In the early fifties and sixties, it was a common sight of boys clad in white *mundu* and shirts with the bundled book and food combo kept on their shoulders moving to schools in groups while girls attired in green skirts and white blouses with cloth bags containing books and food. They represented the archetypal teenagers of the small town.

During the lunch break, when my friends opened their lunch packets, a rare fragrance would emanate from the packets which would water my mouth.

In those days small village hotels also used banana leaves to pack takeaways as an inexpensive packing material. Packed foods had a rare kind of flavor as different curries, pickles, *pappadam*, and fish would be mixed with the leafy taste thus imparting an unusual gastronomic delight. Our ancestors had a profound respect for nature, evident in their ecofriendly way of life, which exemplified their dedication to environmental stewardship. However, with the advent of plastic, polythene, and aluminum foil, the traditional practice of packing food in heated plantain leaves gradually faded into obscurity. Nevertheless, the vibrant memories of this practice remain etched in the collective consciousness of our elders. The aroma of *pothichoru*, carefully wrapped in plantain leaves, and the nostalgic food parcels, still linger in the corridors of our school, evoking a sense of nostalgia and cultural heritage.

11. *Kettu Thengu*: The Pledging of Coconut Palm

Kettu thengu in Malayalam means a pledged coconut tree. In the not-too-distant past it was quite common in Kerala for people from the lower strata of the society to pledge small household items made of brass and copper like *Kindi* (goglet) *Kinnam* (brass plates), *Nilavilakku, Lota, Thambaalam, Uruli,* and such items. These were impoverished urban people from the downtrodden section for whom three square meals a day was a distant dream and lived in abject poverty. For their emergency pecuniary needs, they often approached the rich middle-class families in the village with their prized possessions which may appear trivial to the present generations.

Apart from such inexpensive household articles and jewelry made of gold and silver, people who had coconut trees in their yards used to pledge such fruit-bearing palms as a guarantee for money that they would borrow from the affluent villagers. This practice of pledging coconut palms was quite common among the run-of-the-mill villagers in central Kerala till the mid-seventies and such palms are called *"Kettu Thengu"*. The loan amount depended on the robustness, age, size, and number of coconuts in a bunch. Young palms with plentiful fruits fetched high loans. The one who lends the money would take the harvest month after month till the borrower settles his amount fully. It was a common practice that the coconut plucker would tie the end portion of a coconut frond around the trunk of such *kettu thengu* as an identification mark. Unlike traditional pledging of ornaments or household items that carried high interest rates, palm pledging (*kettu thengu*) was a unique and favorable practice where no interest was required. The crop's yield was sufficient to cover the loan, making it a mutually beneficial arrangement for both the borrower and lender. This aspect made palm pledging a preferred choice for both parties.

We had a couple of such *kettu thengu* under our custody for some money Amma lent out to a family close to her ancestral home. We used to harvest these palms for a few years. Occasionally my youngest sister and I would go there with a coconut plucker and pluck the fruits which would be mostly sold out to the owner or the neighbors for a reasonable amount. I thoroughly enjoyed the visit as the palms were in the middle of a paddy field in a small islet where cattle would be grazing. We used to wade through knee-deep water to the tiny *thuruth* drenching ourselves completely. Since the owner of the palms could not settle his debt even after a long time, Amma after some failed attempts to cajole them to repay the amount finally waived the amount off and returned the palms to the owner much to their delight. She realized that sometimes coercion didn't work. She didn't want to spoil the strong camaraderie between them either.

Later, in the late sixties when the Land Reforms Bill became a reality, most of these coconut groves were divided among the tenants and they became owners of the plots in which they inhabited. Gradually, the system of *kettu thengu* faded into oblivion. True to its appellation coconut palm was then a *"Kalpavriksha"*, practically every part of the tree being used in some way or other, and coconut in its myriad forms has supported the agrarian population of Kerala in bygone decades.

Quite interestingly, perhaps taking a cue from this ancient practice, a few years back Dr Thomas Issac, the then Finance Minister of Kerala, had kickstarted a project that reignited people's interest and enabled farmers to mortgage trees on their land in return for interest-free loans. The first such "tree bank" was established in Meenangadi village of Wayanad district. Plants like mango, jackfruit, and other fruit-bearing indigenous varieties were covered under the scheme. I am unaware of who owns the harvest, and I am also uncertain about the current state of affairs.

12. The Wandering Merchants of Kerala: A Forgotten Genre of Traders

Traveling salesmen were a genre of their own and played a dominant role in the economic development of the state till the early eighties. They came to sell either a product or service.

During my growing up years in a village, I saw peddlers of a wide range used to travel from village to village selling their products. The products they traded ranged from food and clothing to pins and plates which included everything that could be transported as head load.

They traveled long distances, and moved from household to household selling their items. In the interior part of villages which were not connected to the rest of the locality by road and isolated hilly terrains, the travelling salesmen were a common sight engaged in door-to-door sales. They served as bridges between the producers and end users who were separated geographically. They lived in an age very different from ours. The hopes, aspirations, etiquette, culture, and thoughts of that era were different from ours. Their needs were limited. Despite many hardships, they lived a contended life. Simplicity was their forte. There was no electricity, no telephone, no television, no internet, no social media, even a transistor was a luxury then which only very few could afford. Still, they enjoyed life in its totality. I think their story merits narrativization for the posterity to comprehend.

1. *PAPPADAM* SELLER

Once a week, the *pappadakkaran muthalaaly* visited us with his home-made *pappadam*. Normally we purchased 10 *pappadams* costing 25 paise which was sufficient for a week. On special occasions he brought us *mulaku pappadam* (the one with spices) and for Onam he served us jumbo sized *aana pappadam*. He was a stout man of short stature, with a round face and grey hair. Attired in a white *mundu* and an off-white, tailored banyan, he moved at a slow pace, carrying a cotton bag filled with *pappadam*. His legs were severely swollen due to elephantiasis, making every step a laborious effort as he navigated the village alleys with great difficulty Once he told us that he was a classmate of Achan and he always enquired about his wellness. He was a Matriculate with sound knowledge of English and used to clarify the doubts my elder sister on a couple of occasions. Children of the locality liked him much because at times he used to give us *kaarakka* (like jujube fruit). Another reason for the children's adoration for *Muthalaaly* was that he used to procure *Punnakka* (Calophyllum inophyllum seed) from us for which he paid us 5 paisae for a dozen. The seeds, we were told, were used for extracting oil which is believed to have medicinal properties.

2. CLOTHES MERCHANT

Once in a while, a middle-aged man visited our house with a cloth bundle on his head which invariably contained *thorthu* (traditional towel made of coarse white cotton that can be used as wash towel, bath towel or as prestigious towel used in temples for rituals) and *kallimundu*, neatly stacked. On certain times his son also accompanied him with a similar but small bundle atop his head. Amma waited for *Chaliyan*, as he was called, which in fact is a caste of weavers, whenever she wanted to replace old stock of *thorthu* and *mundu*. The *mundu* of different shades and color were neatly piled in the bundle.

3. SELLER OF COPPER WARE

Occasionally, a middle-aged fat man attired in *mundu*, which he folded back above knee level, and a faded banyan came with a large *vaarikotta*, a basket made of pieces of areca nut stem. He would offload the heavy basket in a convenient place like beneath the huge Neem tree in front of Puthanpurackal house so that women from the neighborhood could gather up and buy articles. The merchandise included articles made of brass like *ottuvilakku* (brass kerosene lamps), *kindy* (goglet), *lota* (brass tumbler), *kolamby* (spittoon), *kinnam* (brass plates), *Nilavilakku, vettila thambalam, noottukudam* (*chunnambu kudam*) used for keeping lime paste for betel chewing, incense stick holder and an array of brass utensils. Since he had to carry a heavy load, his stopovers were limited in number, and every stop, he spent a long time to maximize his sales. Festival seasons were field days for him, and he did brisk businesses. For those who couldn't afford to pay the full price upfront, he offered credit options, allowing them to pay in installments during his future visits. Testament to the strong bond of trust he shared with the village women, not a single one defaulted on their payments or cheated him, reflecting a remarkable mutual respect and faith in one another.

4. MERCHANT OF MISCELLANY

E'daakoodam (meaning 'miscellany' or 'mélange' in Malayalam) is a colloquial term used by a peddler to describe himself, indicating that he sells a diverse and assorted collection of goods, a veritable mix of everything.

He would descend on the village once in a blue moon and he would announce his rather unexpected arrival by shouting at high decibel *"e'daakoodam varunnudu pulle"* (*e'daakoodam* is coming guys). He carried a large bamboo basket filled with a plethora of articles like glass bangles, earrings, chains, different types of make-up materials, mirrors, a range of plastic toys, plastic cups, mugs, and sieve to filter tea, *Kumkum*, *Kajal*, *kunjalam* (a hanging hair ornament made of black threads with colorful ornaments) ribbons in a variety of colors, 'Love in Tokyo' hair band, slides, safety pins, saree brooch pin and what not. Once he appeared in the locality the news would spread quickly, women and children would huddle around him in no time. His favorite trading platform was under the shade of the mango tree in our courtyard. I always waited for his arrival because occasionally Amma used to purchase inexpensive toys for me. Along with these articles, he freely traded all kinds of hot news and gossips with the women. He was dark and always appeared in white dhoti and shirt continuously chewing betel. Though past his middle age, he was quite healthy, which he attributed to the regular consumption of tender coconut meat and jaggery during his younger years. Such was his verbiage that even the most skeptics among his clients ran the risk of succumbing to his blandishments.

5. THE EGG SELLER

The egg seller was a constant visitor to the village who came twice a week. He was a tall man who wore unusually thick spectacle. He too had elephantiasis on one leg. He always carried two bagsful of eggs in both hands. Apart from selling, he also used to purchase eggs from households where poultry are reared. Often, we sold eggs to the egg seller which ensured a paltry additional income and rarely did we procure eggs. He kept the eggs of ducks and chicken separate and the former fetched higher price. In our locality most people sold eggs rather than bought them.

6. THE POTTER

Occasionally, the potter from a faraway village appeared with a heavy load of pottery made of clay and laterite. The entire gamut of clay items like *chatty*, *kalam*, *kudam*, plates, money boxes (*kudukka*), and toy utensils were neatly arranged in the huge bamboo basket. He would offload the basket in a convenient place, usually the junction where the village alley was bifurcated. The timing of his visit very often coincided with festive occasions like Onam and Christmas. During each visit, he did brisk business and then quietly disappeared into his next destination.

7. THE KNIFE SHARPENER.

The small town had its own knife sharpener who used to visit our place at irregular intervals. He always carried his foot operated sharpener machine and moved house to house. Women in the neighborhood would huddle around him with their worn-out blunt knives. Sharpening such knives in his *chaana*, the sharpener, gave a new lease of life to them and he charged a small charge for his services.

8. THE TIN PLATING MAN

During sweltering summer days occasionally two middle-aged men used to visit our village yelling in high pitch *"eeyam poosanundo?"*.

Tin plating is a meticulous, intricate, and specialized craft that has been passed down through generations, traditionally practiced by artisans belonging to a specific caste. This labor-intensive process requires great skill and expertise, honed through years of experience and dedication.

Throughout my childhood, two traveling vendors from distant lands would visit our home annually, without fail, typically during the festive season of Onam. Their yearly visits became a cherished tradition, bringing excitement and novelty to our doorstep. During their day-long visit Amma would parade all copper ware like *uruli*, *chembu* (huge copper vessels) of different sizes, copper pots, and a number of copper ware. *Chembotttys*, as they are called locally, would reach in the morning and would start their work. The preliminary steps involve welding the broken vessels. Once this process is done, all the vessels are thoroughly scrubbed and cleaned with caustic soda, followed by an acid wash to get rid of the deposits attached to the container. Then a pit was dug in the ground and a temporary blast furnace was thus formed. Lumps of tin would be melted in a pot by burning coal with continuous blowing using bellows. The molten tin, mixed with some other unknown ingredients, was plated in the interior of the vessels using a piece of cloth shaped like a powder puff. A thin coat was uniformly applied by hand which indeed is a laborious and time-consuming process. This is done to avoid the reaction between acidic foods and copper or brass utensils by providing a protective coating. Tin plating retards this reaction to an extent and thus extended the life of the utensils.

9. THE BUTTERMILK SELLER

The silence of the morning would be broken by the loud calling of *"moru veno moru, Idly chammanthy"* This is the advertisement of Bhai, a middle-aged Tamil woman who sold butter milk and soft, hot and fluffy idly. She spoke in a mixed language of Tamil and Malayalam. She had a couple of buffaloes in her household and she and her family survived on the income from milk, curd, and *idly*. She also used to sell dried cow dung cakes called *chanaka varadi* which were used as fuel for the cremation of dead bodies. Many like her had migrated from neighboring states and made Kochi their second home where they lived in peace and prosperity doing small-time businesses.

10. THE FISH VENDORS

Being a coastal village, fish was available throughout the year. Though there's a big market in the town where vegetables, fruits, fish, and mutton were available aplenty, the women in our neighborhood depended on the fish vendors engaged in door-to-door selling. They came with large bamboo baskets filled to the brim with fresh fish, normally sardines, mackerel and anchovies. These were fish caught from the sea by traditional crafts. On rare occasions, fish caught by small canoes were brought to the landing point near my home. Once the boat arrived, the man in the boat would gently tap on the side of the canoe with a small wooden piece, announcing his arrival. The local people called this *"Chaala kottal"* which means "tapping to announce the arrival of sardines". On hearing the *Chaala kottu*, Amma would ask me to go and purchase some sardines. For 4 Ana, equivalent to the present day 25 paise, we used to get a bagful of sardine which would be more than a kilogram. In those days fish and vegetables were sold in small heaps and system of weighing came into practice only by mid-seventies. The practice of icing was nonexistent. Occasionally fisher women would also visit with their merchandise which ranged from small Pearl Spot (*Karimeen*), *Pallathy* (spotted Etroplus), *Kanambu, Thirutha, Poomeen* and clam meat all of which they caught from the nearby river. Kochumariam used to sell *kakka irachy*, the boiled clam meat, but it was one among the few items which was not allowed in our family as Achan feared that consuming clam meat may cause cholera. His fear was not unfounded as clams were the culprit in many instances of food poisoning. For these poor fisherwomen it was a means of livelihood.

11. THE VEGETABLE VENDORS:

There were a few women who sold fresh vegetables which they either produced themselves or collected from other farms. Among them were spinach, cucumber, bitter gourd, snake gourd, long bean and pumpkin. In our locality, there were many cucumber farms (*Vellari paadam*) that abound in such vegetables. In those days, farming was organic and free of synthetic chemicals, with no use of artificial fertilizers or pesticides. As a result, the vegetables were naturally grown, safe, and bursting with flavor, offering a truly wholesome and delicious experience.

12. THE *LAADA VAIDYAN*

They belonged to a rare genre of visitors who were doctors in their rights selling rare medicines for rare diseases. They claimed it to be similar to Sidha or Unani. The practitioners of such medicines were called *Laada Vaidyans* or *Laada Gurus*. Many of them were quacks who wandered in the villages and cheated many credulous village women with their products and made good their escape without leaving a trail behind. But in the rarest cases, there were instances of *Laada Vaidyan* curing terminally ill people with their magical pills and potions. The *Laada Vaidyans* were mostly from the North and spoke a mixture of Hindi and the local dialect. The gullible villagers ascribed rare healing properties to their concoctions.

13. PALMISTS, ASTROLOGERS AND THE SOOTH SAYERS:

Decades ago, villagers were mired in superstitions and had placed enormous faith in palmistry and astrology. Unsurprisingly, many palmists and astrologers had descended upon the village, exploiting the irrational anxieties and apprehensions of the poor villagers about the future and its uncertainties. Often, the villagers were carried away by the predictions and arcane details of what the future held, always searching for solutions to impending disasters that were highly unlikely to happen. In their fanciful life, they often worried about the many insecurities and uncertainties that life brought. All of us have an innate urge to know about our future, and these palmists and astrologers took advantage of such deep-rooted notions.

The village was also frequented by many other small-time merchants and service providers like the Tamil women who polished the grinding stone, the man selling vinegar, the merchant of tamarind, the cotton candy seller, the ice candy seller, the merchant of *payasam*, the old man who repaired umbrellas, the young man who repaired damaged footwear, the old woman who sold i*dly* and *sambar* every morning and the perfume seller. All these small-time vendors and service providers, who made an otherwise monotonous and arduous village life more bearable and enjoyable, had once sustained the life of the villagers. While many were regulars some were infrequent visitors and a few among them appeared only once in a blue moon. The villagers, however, established a friendly bond with these travelling salesmen who sold either goods or services. In a bygone period, they were the cultural ambassadors of the landscape. However, the emergence of modern trade practices such as digital marketing and e-commerce have almost completely erased them from the rural landscape.

13. Christmas In Kochi: Rose-Tinted Memories of a Colorful Period

Christmas and New Year are occasions that are celebrated in Kochi with grandeur in an atmosphere filled with *joie de vivre*. These are occasions that exude considerable fervor and immense gaiety among the populace. The cozy hangover of the colonial era is still lingering in the breeze of Kochi which bestows an ethereal old-world charm to the atmosphere. The occasion marks the nostalgic confluence of history, culture, and tradition.

In the mid-seventies, we used to celebrate Christmas and New Year in a way that is beyond the imagination of the present generation. There were several groups like those of children, young boys and girls, women, men, and the aged, who engaged in a plethora of activities related to the celebrations, each one with specific responsibilities.

Winter in Kerala is a brief but delightful time sandwiched between a strong and ferocious monsoon and a scorching summer. Cool and serene winter dusks provide an ideal setting for Xmas and New Year celebrations.

The entire small town, adorned with stars and illuminating light, would wear a festive look. We, the children, eagerly waited for the commencement of Xmas vacation. In those days homemade stars were the sole option and each household made Xmas stars on its own with unique sizes and shapes. The making of Xmas stars was an art in itself, a task in which children would be generously assisted by the elders. First, a skeleton of the star is made using dried and sliced bamboo stems. The frame would be pasted with glossy papers of varying colors. Long tails made of paper streamers would be attached to the star's corners.

"*Aakasa vilakku*" which means "sky lantern" is a unique version of a decorative lamp used as a substitute for stars in some places. It is comparatively larger with a long cylindrical body of 3-4 feet with many sides. The top and bottom of the *aakasa vilakku* would be open and would be embellished with outwardly projecting overhangs beautifully decorated with paper frills. A lot of painstaking labor, patience and passion contribute to the making of *aakasa vilakku*. They also come in global and crystal shapes. I have seen similar sky lanterns in Goa also, perhaps a relic of the Portuguese era. By nightfall, stars and *aakasa vilakku* would be illuminated with small lighted kerosene lamps. After carefully placing the lighted lamp inside, the star would be gently hoisted using coir ropes, either on a long mast or on tree tops, a sight we profoundly relished. We roamed around the neighborhood to have a glimpse of this spectacular sight of "star rise" enjoying the cold breeze of winter dusks. Unexpected winter rains used to dampen both the stars and our enthusiasm. Once the celebration was over, the frame of these stars and sky lanterns would be kept safely in some corners of the house to be used in the coming years.

The construction of the cribs would be the prerogative of the elders which housed clay figurines of the infant Jesus, Joseph and Mary along with miniature statues of three wise men. A few shepherds and their sheep, huddled around, would complement the crib. Angels would dangle from the hut tops amongst stars.

A small tree adorned with glittering festoons, small stars and color paper would incarnate as a Xmas tree.

In many houses, the soft stem of plantain after removing the outer layers of skin (*Vazha pindy*) would be decorated with colorful flags with their long sticks deeply stuck to the stem. To add glory to the structure, around the stem small circular rings made of *eerkkil* (the dried midrib of coconut leaf) would be stuck. Upon each ring, a small kerosene lamp would be placed, with a large one on top of the plantain stem. When lit, golden yellow light emanated from them, which imparted an unearthly charm to the surrounding area. These kerosene lamps would continue to burn smoldering black smoke till daybreak. All these illuminations would continue till New Year.

The high point of Xmas was the array of ethnic delicacies like *Vellayappam* and stew, *Vattayappam*, *Kuzhalappam*, and *Avalosunda* which would be gifted to us on Xmas Eve by our Christian neighbors.

During these days small groups of Carols would visit us attired as Santa. They moved from house to house singing and dancing to the tune of drums which would fill us with thrills and spills.

Grown-up boys would stage short skits, usually Biblical stories lasting 5-10 minutes. They would appear with their paraphernalia including a background curtain, (usually an old sari or bed sheet) held tightly on both ends by two boys, a front curtain of a similar kind and a large hurricane lamp. They would be rewarded with ten to twenty-five paise depending on the perfection of their performance. We used to accompany the troupe to all the neighboring houses which they visited and by the end, the dialogues became by heart for us. The more professional troupes used more refined props like attractive lights and glittering background curtains of better nature. A petromax placed inside an empty tea chest with an opening in the front where an array of colored transparent plastic papers was placed on a rotating frame, provided a multicolor visual treat for the audience, numbering a dozen or so. For us, Xmas and New Year were secular festivals that we celebrated with equal zeal and enthusiasm. Beyond the barriers of caste, class and culture we cohabitated cheek by jowl.

The midnight Mass on Xmas Eve was a boisterously merry occasion as children and grown-ups enthusiastically thronged the nearby church in the village. We used to watch the people moving in small groups to the church through the village alleys braving the chilling wintery breeze.

The fortnight-long Christmas-New Year celebration would come to a magnificent finale with the famed *Pappanji Kali* (*Pappanji* is a Portuguese term meaning 'grandpa'), a pageantry involving music bands, men and children in fancy dress, and tableaux. By nightfall, these processions would originate from different parts of old Kochi, culminating at Fort Kochi parade ground where the smaller processions would merge into a mammoth one. The burning of *Pappanji* at midnight, symbolizing bidding adieu to the past year and welcoming the New Year, would mark the end of the season's celebrations. By the early eighties, the localized New Year processions were replaced with the present Cochin Carnival, which has become a major tourist attraction for Kochi and neighboring areas

14. Vibrant Village Ponds

We often recollect those idyllically happy and halcyon days of our childhood with great enthusiasm. Presently, my thoughts are centered around ponds which were once an integral part of our village life and culture.

Ponds played crucial roles in the life and culture of our village. Till a few decades ago our village was abounding with a plethora of ponds. In the olden days, almost all households had their ponds which catered to everyday needs for drinking water and also for irrigating the farms.

These perennial ponds were constantly replenished by rainfall, serving as a reliable source of water throughout the year. The village ponds played a crucial dual role, mitigating floodwaters during the monsoon season and providing a steady supply for irrigation during the dry summer months, thereby ensuring a stable water balance in the village ecosystem.

Ponds were an integral part of temples and *Kavus*. While a huge pond (*ambalakkulam*) in the North-Eastern part of the front courtyard is an unavoidable feature of temples, the *Kavus* accommodated a number of them which vary in numbers and sizes in accordance with the vastness of the *Kavus*. Those ponds, which were home to many water plants, fishes and birds, formed an integrated ecosystem. The ponds would be fringed by dense thickets of various types of medicinal trees and shrubs which provided hiding places for birds and animals. The water percolating through the roots of such trees eventually got collected in the ponds and the devout believers had deep faith in their medicinal properties. It was for this reason that people used to take ritualistic dips in temple ponds during special occasions. They worshipped temple ponds with awe and devotion. During annual temple festivals it was in the temple ponds that the ritualistic holy dip of deity, the *aaraattu* is performed. Normally the temple ponds would be protected by a wall or barbed wire fence that surrounded the pond perimeters.

Annually, as a tradition, the temple ponds would undergo a thorough maintenance routine before the festive season, where they would be completely drained and scrubbed clean of accumulated silt and mud, allowing for a refreshing recharge with crystal-clear water, revitalizing the sacred spaces for the upcoming celebrations.

There was a large pond in the North-Eastern corner of Sree Bhavaneeswara Temple near our school. In the olden days, the ponds were cleaned up by laborers who belonged to a particular caste. They accomplished the task in a systematic manner. The team comprising twenty to twenty-five laborers would drain the water using a large cone shaped bamboo basket, the *the'kku kutta* to the accompaniment fascinating folk songs called *the'kku paattu*, which reflected the cultural ethos of a generation. We, the children, thoroughly enjoyed the draining and cleaning of the vast temple pond. The drain water carried along many fish, such as Climbing Perch *(Karooppu)* and Snakehead *(Varaal)*, both of which could survive out of water for long. Within a couple of days after draining, the water would be recharged naturally reaching its original level. A flight of steps led to the bathing ghats where people used to wash their hands and feet before entering the temple. All temple ponds that I have seen had a ubiquitous greenish color imparted by certain algae. By the late sixties the practice of manual draining of temple ponds had been replaced with pumps driven by motors which indeed has taken away much of the thrill and charm of the pond cleaning.

We had a large pond in the North-Eastern corner of our homestead. Till the mid-seventies, this pond remained the main source of drinking water in our locality. People from the immediate neighborhood would come to collect water. The pond surface was completely carpeted with a thick layer of water cabbage (*kula paayal*). During the rainy season, the water would breach the barrier and overflow to the front courtyard bringing with them a lot of fish. It was a fascinating sight to see the white-breasted water hen known in Malayalam as *kulakkozhi*, which inhabited the adjoining bamboo thickets, walking gleefully over the water's surface.

Later with the arrival of piped drinking water the ancient pond became a victim of neglect and a few years ago it was unceremoniously filled up to build a house for my nephew. Along with the pond, the water hens too vanished forever forming part of our collective memory.

Fast-paced urbanization has killed the once ubiquitous village ponds which were completely erased from the landscape. Thus, we lost open reservoirs for collecting rainwater leading to frequent flooding after heavy rains and during hot summer months exacerbating the shortage of potable water. Only the temple ponds survived the onslaughts because of the sanctity and traditional beliefs attached to them. Claude Monet, the French painter, once remarked, "All of a sudden I had the revelation of how enchanting my pond was."

15. Requiem For a Grandma Tree

A huge *Vaalan pulimaram*, the tamarind tree, stood at the edge of the courtyard of my wife's ancestral home with its tiny fallen leaves spread across the courtyard. All through the year, the tree bore fruits in good amounts. She's indeed more than a century old tree as testified by the elders in the family. The enormity and spread of the tree had been awesome. Once, a few years ago, she had been struck by lightning and ignited a fire which was then put out with the help of Fire Service personnel. Despite this, she continued to exist unfazed, unharmed and unaffected by the unexpected event, showing her indomitable spirit of survival. She had been a symbol of remarkable fortitude and admirable hope which we humans should emulate.

She stood there all these years with her canopy spread throughout the compound, sheltering the courtyard from the hot summer sun. The roots had been spread across the immediate vicinity and a part of the branches extended out to the nearby road which overarched the passing High Tension power line.

Family members spanning four generations have been blessed with the cool comfort of the grandma tree. While toddlers had their exciting first solo and unsteady steps underneath the grandma tree, growing up children clamored and played under her cool shade; she might have enjoyed all those memorable days herself. Like us, trees too have emotions and feelings. She was a silent witness to all the happenings, whether good, bad or unpleasant which happened in the family. The monumental tree had been a silent witness of history. It was under the vastness of her shade that a huge Pandal was erected for our marriage in the late eighties. It was again under her shade the bodies of grandmother-in-law, father-in-law, mother-in-law and recently the younger brother-in-law were kept for paying last respects before funeral service. The joys and sorrows, pangs and pleasures, trials and tribulations, prosperity and hardships; she witnessed in silence everything with equal grittiness and endurance. She taught us the moral that we should face all obstacles and blessings in our lives with equal composure.

When the family property was divided as per the will executed by my wife's parents, she inherited the plot in front of the many decades-old *tharavad*, which extended up to the eastern boundary. When the partition became a reality, we became the owners of the ancient tree. However, a considerable portion of her branches were spread over the old house causing damage to the roof during the rainy season. The new owners of the house persistently requested us to cut and remove the tree to provide a lasting solution to a perennial problem. The branches that touched the power line were also a cause of concern for us. Finally, though rather hesitantly, we decided to cut her down. And a year ago, she became a victim to the tree cutter's saw, permanently wiping out the cool shade she provided all these years. When she fell, along with her, many birds and insects that inhabited the tree suddenly became homeless. Nobody bade a fitting farewell to her, nor anyone feel the need to embrace her for one last time. We even forgot to take a picture of her to keep it as a souvenir, a framed memory. Had we left her unharmed, she would have survived many more years.

"Trees are poems that earth writes upon the sky".
Khalil Gibran.

"To be without trees would, in the most literal way, to be without our roots".
Richard Mabey.

16. *Manappadam:* My First Encyclopedia

By the time I reached second standard, our class teacher suggested that we get a copy of the *Manappadam* which was available in the small shack selling sweets and notebooks across the school.

Heeding her advice, I purchased one for 5 paise. This was the first ever reference book I used in my life.

Titled *"Koothoorinte Vistruta Manappadam"*, it was indeed a small booklet with some 30 pages or so. The book was printed on a yellowish-tinted cheap quality paper and the print quality was also equally inferior. However, I liked the book very much for reasons unknown to me. When opened the book, a smell of freshly cut raw arecanut emanated from its pages. The front and back covers were printed in color. On the front cover was a multicolored geographical map of India with each state printed in a different color using green, yellow and red with light blue for the seas. I vaguely remember that the contours of our country especially the North-East were vastly different from what we see today. I think the Pak-Occupied Kashmir was depicted on the map as an integral part of our country. It was printed in Malayalam. On the back cover, there was a map of Kerala which at that time extended from Gokarnam in the

North to Kanyakumari in the South. Years later, in a territorial rearrangement, Kanyakumari was ceded to Tamil Nadu, while Gokarnam was allocated to Karnataka, in exchange for Palakkad, marking a significant redrawing of state boundaries.

In later editions, the front cover image was updated to showcase a visual representation of various weights and measures, arranged in a descending order of value, with the largest unit at the base. Accompanying this illustration were images of all the coins in circulation at the time, including denominations of 1, 2, 3, 5, 10, 20, 25, and 50 paise, as well as the 1-rupee coin, providing a comprehensive visual guide to the country's currency and measurement systems.

The contents invariably included basics of language, beginning with the alphabets of Malayalam, English and Hindi. This was followed by numbers from 1 to 100 in Roman, Hindi and Malayalam. The present generation may be surprised to know that we have numerals in Malayalam which were once used commonly in communication. Even now we can see such Malayalam numerals as page numbers in old copies of epics like *Ramayanam* and *Panchangam*.

The booklet included multiplication tables from 2 to 10, a basic conversion table for weights and measures, and essential mathematical formulas for area and volume. There was a section dedicated to Malayalam idioms and phrases, along with elementary Malayalam grammar. It also featured the names of months according to the Gregorian, *Saka*, and Malayalam calendars, the twenty-eight stars of the Malayalam almanac, and a small section on home remedies. In the early sixties, we treated this booklet as our encyclopedia and a ready reckoner for multiplication tables. Today, in hindsight, I greatly cherish those memories of the *Vistruta Manappadari* and the vital information it provided during my primary school days.

17. Village Vistas

My village life provided enough to enjoy the rustic charm and qualities ascribed to life in a countryside. The villagers were honest and unpretentious, and they led a simple but enjoyable life.

In my younger days, the whole family depended on the paltry salary that my father earned. Amma used to wait anxiously for the postman who bought the money order every month. This amount was hardly sufficient to meet the day-to-day expenses of the family for a month and put us in a penurious situation. Though our life had been through many vicissitudes she encountered them with patience and uncommon composure. She was ready to travel the extra mile for the sake of our wellbeing. To earn some additional income Amma engaged herself in activities like raising poultry.

Rearing hens was an arduous task, and the process began with the selection of eggs. The first thing she did was to select eggs that were fertilized. From a clutch of 30 or so eggs, she selected the fertile ones and for this, she employed a crude method which was quite popular in those days. The chosen egg was positioned upright with the pointed end facing upwards. Next, a small metal tool, typically a knife, was held horizontally with one end gently touching the top of the egg. If the egg was fertile, it would slowly rotate, and those eggs were selected for incubation and hatching. Others were removed. I don't know the science behind this method but every time it worked with astonishing accuracy. With a small piece of carbon, she then drew a cross meticulously along the length of each egg thus selected, the purpose of which is still a mystery. She might have done this as a way to know the position of the eggs in the "incubator "because every few days the eggs have to be rotated gently to ensure uniform heating. The eggs were then carefully placed inside a wide-mouthed clay pan padded with coconut fiber. The broody hen *(porunna kozhi)* was then allowed to sit over the eggs and incubate them. The dedicated hen sat patiently and continuously for 20-21 days till the eggs hatched. We were flabbergasted at the sight of the hatchlings trying to come out of the shells by breaking open them with their tiny beaks.

When the newly hatched chicks were one or two weeks old, Amma would make a hanging cage called *"vallam"* to keep them safe. The improvised cage was made of *'oala'*, the thatched coconut leaves, with a base made of *'ali'*, the dried midrib of coconut frond, which formed a network at the bottom. All four sides were covered with *oala* which gradually tapered towards the top leaving an opening large enough to put one's hand inside. The top of the *vallam* would be tied to a long rope the other end of which would be passed through a curved iron rod tied firmly to a tree. By evening Amma would put all chicks one by one carefully into the *vallam* disregarding the vociferous protests of mother hen. Once this exercise is over, she would gently lift the *vallam* to a height of 5-6 feet above the ground. This provided security for the chicken from stray dogs and the Palm Civet *(marapatty)* which were common in those days, looking for an easy meal. I reveled in the responsibility of lifting the *vallam* and took turns with my elder sister to accomplish this coveted task. Similarly, the process of carefully lowering the *vallam* in the early morning hours was equally captivating and a delightful experience.

My grandson Alekh's enthusiasm for chickens and domestic animals has rekindled my own childhood memories, bridging experiences across generations.

18. Ruminations on Sibling Relationship

During our lifetime, we experience various relationships with differing intensity and sensitivity. Have you ever wondered what the most marvelous relationships in a person's life are? Undoubtedly, the most wonderful of all human relationships is the one with our parents. Following this, we encounter a wide range of relationships, each with its own emotional hues, including those between spouses, siblings, parents and children, friends, relatives, colleagues, and many more. Of all these relationships, the bond between siblings during their formative years is perhaps the most endearing, leaving an indelible mark on a person's psyche that lasts a lifetime. I am in awe of the preciousness and strength of these innocent and unbridled connections. Truly blessed are those who have the privilege of growing up alongside their siblings, forging memories and experiences that shape their lives forever. Most people of my generation were born and raised in large families with many siblings. I am blessed with five siblings, including three lovely sisters and two adorable brothers, who showered me with immense love, care, and a great deal of empathy. This profound empathy stemmed from the ravages of diseases that were my constant childhood companions, leaving deep scars on my mind and body. As the youngest of six children, I enjoyed special privileges and immunity from capricious whims. Perhaps because all my siblings were much older than me, I was a victim of excessive pampering, which made me an arrogant and opinionated child. By the time I was born in November 1961, my parents had already passed their middle age and in a sense, I was an accidental child. My eldest sister Valsala and eldest brother Siva Prasad belong to an early generation. At the time of my birth, my eldest sister had reached 21 and at the time of her marriage, I was hardly two. All my siblings treated me with parent-like care and affection and thus I spent my early childhood days in a quaint and quiet village enjoying the rustic charm and innocence. I was brought up like a little prince, a luxury not available to my elder sisters and brothers. My elder brother Rajiv used to comment in a lighter vein that while I was fed with Horlicks and Bournvita, (two famous health drink brands), they survived on rice gruel (*kanjivellam*). What he said was partly true because, during their childhood days, the entire family of 5 children and parents solely depended on the modest salary of Achan. They lived in penury and Amma engaged in some part-time activities like goat farming, selling firewood and poultry farming in a small way to supplement the family income in her way. She earned a paltry amount from her modest enterprise. Life had always been a roller coaster ride for her with unexpected twists and turns. By the time I was born, our financial situation had somewhat stabilized and Achan had reached a position of higher rank in the Air Force. Amma used to tell her neighborhood friends and close relatives that my birth, though belated, had heralded good fortune in the family as it was exactly on the same day I was born, that my eldest brother got his much-anticipated appointment in the Air Force. Achan and Amma ascribed the newfound job of their eldest son as a blessing to the youngest nascent boy and considered the coincidence as a happy augury in the family. However, I harbor no such sentiments and do not wish to claim credit for the fortunate developments. Similarly, I do not accept responsibility for any unfortunate events that have occurred in our family since my arrival.

Since all, except the youngest sister Sheela, were much older than me I was denied opportunities to engage in games and play with them, for I was too young for them to make a perfect playmate to play around. They, instead, treated me like a child of their own. It was only with the youngest sister, who was older by seven years, that I shared my brotherly affection and adolescent feelings. Together we used to play various village games. Though we fought with each other frequently for no particular reason, there was bonhomie amongst us, and she carefully looked after me during my primary school days with motherly affection. She was a good storyteller too whose bedtime narratives I thoroughly enjoyed. On a couple of occasions, she had gone for a movie with her neighborhood friends the stories of which she later narrated to me with her generous additions. She was trained in classical music for a few years under the tutelage of Raman Kutty Bhagavathar, the earliest guru of legendary singer K J Yesudas, and even today she sings superbly in her mellifluous voice. She never misses an opportunity to prove her musical prowess.

By the time I turned five both my brothers had joined the Air Force, the eldest sister had already been married off, Achan had been posted in faraway places and I gleefully spent my childhood days with Amma and two elder sisters Anandam and Sheela. Amma was always burdened with her familial responsibilities. She was often troubled by rheumatism, and the elephantiasis on her right leg had a crippling effect on her health and movement. During those early years, when Amma was tormented by endless health issues, it was my second sister Anandam who cared for, loved, and nurtured me. Whenever I fell ill, which was of common occurrence, it was she who always took the initiative of taking me to the doctor. For minor ailments either Anchal Master or Raghavan *Vaidyar*, the village clinicians, were consulted while for diseases of a more serious nature, I was taken to Dr Xavier of Hilda Clinic who administered "English" medicines. She was an excellent cook with amazing culinary skills. The keeper of stories and secrets, her loud laughter echoed through our home. Delicious non-vegetarian foods like fish and mutton curry which she prepared had been a gastronomic delight. Finger foods such as sugar-coated diamond cuts, *achappam*, *pakkavada* and *avalose podi* were her special forte. Amongst all the six children of my parents, it was she who toiled a lot in life and she was also the one with the shortest lifespan. I still retain wonderful memories of the days of her marriage in the early seventies which I greatly savored and celebrated. The preparations for the marriage started almost a month in advance. The house was abuzz with various activities like painting and whitewashing the house by Kochappan, mending the thatched fence under the leadership of Krishnan *Velan*, the preparation of land by weeding out thickets of wild growth by Chori *Pulayan* and his assistant, preparation of mouthwatering Halwa and Laddu by Velayudhan Chettan and his two sons, *eeyam poosal* of copper utensils and a lot more. A couple of days before the ceremony a splendid and spacious Pandal was erected in the front courtyard by George Nangeri and Co., the leading decorators of the day. The Pandal was decorated on all sides using *cheenaveli*, panels made of braided bamboo reeds while the top was adorned with white cloth embellished with decoration. A portion of the Pandal on the northern side was modified into the *kalavara*, the temporary kitchen for preparing the *sadya*.

When Anandam left after marriage to Edappally to join her in-laws, Amma used to lament that the home had fallen asleep. It was always her boisterous talks and loud laughter that enlivened our days. Her evening prayer was a wonderful vociferous experience. Even our distant neighbors used to tell us that Anandam's high-decibel chanting of evening prayer, *namajapam*, could be audible to them. During those years in the early seventies, a journey to Edappally by bus was a pleasure trip worth enjoying. Occasionally, Amma used to visit her daughter and two grandchildren and she would take me along. The fascinating trip in itself was cause for considerable excitement. The sumptuous lunch and evening tea with a variety of finger foods which she served added to my excitement. I enjoyed every moment of that journey lasting one and a half hours. In those days bus services to interior parts like Cheranelloor, near Edappally, were limited and we went by Wilsy which plied in Kumbalangi-Cheranelloor route, in its morning trip. We returned by the same bus in the evening after spending a few wonderful hours with her. Sukumaran, her husband always accompanied us to the bus stop.

On another occasion, I stayed with her at her Chettiparambu residence as part of a two-week-long treatment for my asthma using an *ottamooli* (panacea). Though my disease remained unabated, my brief stay gave me a fascinating experience for me to relish in my later life. Whenever she got a chance to visit our home she would come here and spend a few days with us. Sukumaran, her husband, too had great respect and adoration for Achan and Amma. Those were the best years in her life and back then her husband had a lucrative coconut oil business in the town. But things took a sudden turn for the worse with the unexpected closure of Sree Bhadra Oil Mills, from where he sourced coconut oil. My sister's later life was marked by abject poverty, and to make ends meet, she engaged in a plethora of activities. However, businesses like a small kiosk near Edappally railway station, a small restaurant attached to her house at Edappally, and finally a small, nondescript provision store on our ancestral land, which Achan had gifted her in the backyard of our family house, never guaranteed a comfortable return worth the effort. In hindsight, I feel that life had never been fair to her. With the sudden passing of her husband, she found herself going through a tough time and she felt as though she had lost life's moorings. The day after her husband's unfortunate death when I visited her, she looked lost in deep thoughts and she appeared to me like frozen pathos, a sight I cannot forget. After the marriage of her daughter, she was trying hard to survive along with her son. Things seemed to be proceeding quietly on expected lines. But fate has something else for her. 18th April 2002 was like any other day in her life. She came to visit my daughter at the hospital where she had a surgery on that day. But by evening I was greeted with the shocking news about her sudden death. The news of her sudden and untimely demise left me petrified. It took some time for me to come to terms with the reality. She suffered many trials and tribulations in her short life. When she died, she was fifty-four, the youngest person to die in our family. The sudden and untimely death of their beloved daughter had emotionally shattered both Achan and Amma. She left leaving behind a feast of sweet memories to relish later in my life. For me, she was more than an elder sister, for she loved me with a motherly affection.

THERE IS NOTHING QUITE TREASURED AS THE CHILDHOOD MEMORIES WE MAKE WITH OUR SIBLINGS.

Anonymous

19. Ambujakshy: A Chef Extraordinaire and Her Culinary Excellence

In a traditional Kerala culinary landscape dominated by men, this woman stood out as a pioneering chef, making significant contributions to the preservation and promotion of authentic Kerala cuisine. Her expertise and dedication earned her widespread recognition and acclaim, shattering gender barriers in the process. When I first met Ambujakshy over five decades ago, she was already in her fifties. Although I don't recall the exact circumstances of our initial encounter, I vividly remember that it was in the *kalavara* at a neighborhood wedding reception. What struck me was the universal respect with which people of all ages, from young children to elderly individuals, addressed her as Ambujakshy Chechi. She was a stout and outspoken woman who left a lasting impression on me. She had by then earned her reputation as a wonderful cook with unmatched culinary skills and her culinary service was an inevitable requirement for every marriage ceremony in our village during the seventies and eighties. She prepared delicious vegetarian *sadya* comprising a whole array of foods ranging from fried banana chips to *pappadam, pazham* and *payasam* which satiated the palates of all her guests. The number of items served varied from a dozen to more than twenty, depending on the social status of the marriage party.

She had always been accompanied by a couple of her assistants, a middle-aged man and a woman slightly younger than her. She was a trailblazer, shattering gender barriers as the first and only woman in a male-dominated field. Her culinary skills were a stark contrast to the bland cooking of her predecessors, which was tactfully referred to as 'Nala Pachakam' (a euphemism for cooking by men).

She would arrive at the wedding venue by mid-afternoon, a day before the ceremony, to take charge of the *kalavara*, the makeshift kitchen set up adjacent to the main Pandal. With her trusty assistants by her side, she would meticulously ensure that every item on her extensive ingredient list was procured and ready for the grand feast ahead.

Then the utensils needed such as a couple of huge *uruli*, the traditional cauldron made of brass, and *vaarpu*, made of copper, would be washed and cleaned thoroughly. The bottom of these utensils would be smeared with a coat of ash paste. This was for the easy cleaning of the soot and carbon from the underbelly of the utensils after use. In those days the hearths were fueled with firewood, which invariably left a thick deposit of soot and carbon which was removed laboriously.

The kitchen would be opened ceremoniously by heating the empty *uruli* atop a huge temporary hearth, with prayers and elders in the family would offer coins into the *uruli* as *dakshina* to propitiate Annapoorneshwari, the Goddesses of *Annam* (food). This amount belonged to the cook which Ambujakshy Chechi would collect and keep in her purse.

From then on, she would be at the helm of the kitchen and would give instructions one after another to her assistants and also to the numerous women from the neighborhood who had huddled to partake in the elaborate preparations. Back then the preparation of a *sadya* was a community event where people from the neighboring houses and close relatives took part in what is called *"sramadanam"*, which means voluntary service in the form of labor. Those women would put in their efforts to cut the various vegetables to pieces, scrape the coconut, and grind the shredded coconut into a fine paste in grinding stones (*ammikallu*). There would be several wooden coconut scrapers (*chirava*) and grinding stones collected from the neighbors and nearby relatives. Cutting vegetables for various culinary items like *aviyal, sambar, koottukari, kattiparippu* and peeling and slicing ginger, garlic, onion and shallot would be a grueling and time-consuming task in which everyone would take part. During the nightlong preparations of the *sadya* the kitchen would be abuzz till morning with a clamoring crowd.

Actual cooking would commence by evening with the frying of banana chips and *upperi*. This would be followed by other curries like pickles, *puli inchi, ullicurry, pulisserry, rasam* and *sambar* in that order. Items like *parippu, aviyal, payasam* and rice, which had very short shelf life, would be prepared only in the early morning. The contents in the *uruli* and *vaarpu* were stirred using a broad iron spatula with a very long wooden handle called *chattukam*, also called *nayanpu* which resembled a paddle. This laborious process was normally carried out by her male assistant though she would also participate actively. When the food was ready, the contents of the *uruli* would be transferred to big storage vessels using large scoops made of dried arecanut spathe. After making each curry this process would be repeated due to the difficulty of removing the hot *uruli* from the burning hearth after making each item. The frying of *pappadam* in oil would mark the culmination of a backbreaking job that would last overnight. Till the last item was ready, Ambujakshy would remain active throughout the night giving instructions to her assistants, tasting the items under preparation, suggesting modifications like adding some turmeric or salt or some other ingredients and lowering the flame, and occasionally passing some innocuous comments. A petromax lamp would be hung in the corner of the kitchen, its whizzing sound audible from far away, breaking the silence of the night, as electricity had not reached our village until the mid-seventies. In between her backbreaking work, Ambujakshy would gulp down a few glasses of black tea, followed by noisy belches. She would check the quality and quantity of each item till she is fully satisfied with both. For her this was no time to rest or take a break

By daybreak, the elaborate cooking process would be completed. The cooked rice would be strained off water and would be spread over bamboo mats with a lighted *Nilavilakku* on one side.

Now it was time for Ambujakshy to rest for a few minutes after backbreaking chores and later after her morning routine, she would be ready in the kitchen. She would supervise the way different items were arranged in small serving containers in the order they were being served. In the past, the traditional Kerala *sadya* was served on the floor, where plantain leaves were laid out on a tarpaulin-lined surface. Guests would sit on screw pine mats to enjoy their meal. However, by the early 1970s, the use of tables and chairs had become increasingly prevalent, marking a shift away from this traditional dining setup. She would stand in a corner of the kitchen and oversee the serving of the *sadya* until it was completed. During such time, tension was visible on her face because if any item ran out of stock, she would have to face the music from the marriage party. But seldom did her reckoning go wrong. Gradually, her name and fame spread beyond our village for her gastronomic delight, and she was invited by people from neighboring villages to cook which was a true recognition of her talents as a marvelous cook. Perfection of her cooking was in her wonderful recipes. Ambujakshy was an excellent culinary maestro, and her culinary vision was great indeed. She exuded a captivating and invigorating presence. She was a wonderful and flamboyant woman who brought grace and dignity to her profession. She died a few years ago. Her story is a wonderful reminder of the enduring legacy of a woman in the culinary history and tradition of Kerala.

*EATING IS A NECESSITY
BUT COOKING IS AN ART.*
Georges Auguste Escoffier

20. Parambikkulam: A Journey to Tranquility

To take a break from the monotony of routine, we embarked on a trip to Parambikkulam Tiger Reserve (PTR), a natural world surrounded by its beauty and serenity, along with the extended family from my wife's side. We had been planning this sojourn for the past month.

Located in the Western Ghats, Parambikkulam Tiger Reserve is an ancient mountain system with its resources and ecosystem benefits being shared by five South Indian states. For Kerala, Sahyadri is a benefactor and protector, supporting and sustaining human existence in this ecologically fragile state.

Our original itinerary was to access Parambikkulam through the meandering forest path that passes through hilly terrains of tourist locales such as Thumboormoozhy, Athirappally, Vazhachal, Malakkappara and Sholayar. Though arduous and time-consuming, we were told by regular commuters that this route would provide an opportunity to enjoy the picturesque views of the forests with fairly good chances of sighting wildlife at close range. However, we had to curtail our journey at Vazhachal as the road ahead was under repair, which played spoilsport with our plan.

We were unperturbed by the unexpected stumbling block which had not dampen our enthusiasm. We decided to take a detour and continue the rest of our journey through the Pollachy route. Braving the hot and humid summer weather, we travelled through Tamil Nadu for a few miles before entering the Kerala border. On the way we had a sumptuous lunch which we took along with us.

Anappady is the gateway of the Parambikkulam Tiger Reserve where we reached by 3-pm. In contrast to the sweltering heat in Kerala, we were pleasantly welcomed by the cool and serene climate of the sanctuary.

The enchanting landscape has captivated us. Kaliyappan, a seasoned forest guide with fairly good knowledge about the sanctuary and its wild inhabitants, was waiting for us.

After a grueling and exhausting journey, we were all drained. So, we revitalized ourselves with a refreshing hot tea session, surrounded by mischievous monkeys that added a playful touch to our much-needed break.

Kaliyappan was a quintessential guide with mastery of language and deep knowledge of the flora and fauna of the forest. He assiduously pointed out the features of each animal we encountered. Our accommodation was at Bison Valley, around 20 Km away from Anappady. He suggested us to visit a few places before checking in to the IB of the forest department. Normally, private vehicles are allowed only up to Anappady and for jungle rides one has to depend on the vehicle being arranged by the forest department. The luxury of travelling in the comfort of own vehicles to loiter around was a privilege available only to those who stay overnight.

Our first destination, Thunakadav Dam, was an earthen dam built across Thunakadav river. On the way, Kaliyappan turned vocal and our curiosity prompted him to give a detailed narrative about the forest and its dwellers. With childlike inquisitiveness, I noted down the important points of his description.

I picked up some key points from his conversation, which was a unique mix of Malayalam and Tamil, reflecting the linguistic diversity of the region.

Parambikkulam was declared as Tiger Reserve in 2010 which then had an area of 285 sq Km. Later, the area was extended to 643 Sq Km. Tourists are allowed only in the periphery of the vast forest referred to as a buffer zone while the core zone is beyond the reach of visitors, where animals and birds of various species roam around freely. Parambikkulam Sanctuary is the 38th tiger reserve in India. In 2010 there were only 19 tigers out of 1700 in India. Currently, Parambikkulam has 38 of 2226 tigers in the country. The 2018 census released by the Prime Minister in April 2023 reinforces his statement according to which PTR has a population in the range of 28 to 35 of 3167 tigers in India.

Like our fingerprint, the stripes of each tiger are unique and tigers are identified by the stripes. Unlike other wild animals, tigers have well-defined zones and within 20 Km one can spot only a single tiger. However, when food is scarce the zone may be expanded to 40 Km. Like domestic dogs, the tigers scent marks their zones by urinating. Tigers are nocturnal animals and hunt during the night, Indian gaur being their favorite food. A fully mature tiger weighs 200-250 Kg but can easily overpower and kill an Indian gaur of 600 Kg. Even the mighty elephants are not spared. Tigers have a penchant for large prey. With a single lethal strike, it can kill an Indian gaur of double its size. Once the tiger kills a prey it will not eat it immediately or in a single gulp. Rather the tiger will take the visceral mass out and allow it to decay for a few days usually 4 to 7. Then it savors the decomposed food slowly which will last for several days. The tiger will search for another prey only after finishing the available food. As a rule, a tiger will not attack small animals as it does not want to waste the sharpness of its teeth which have only limited life. Normally, on average, a tiger will eat 30 animals in a year and it can live without food for many days. The strange feeding habits of tigers astonished us. I could see several signages displayed by the forest department with the slogan "Save the stripes", obviously a campaign underscoring the need to protect the big cats from human interventions.

The main mating season of tigers is from November to January and has a gestation period of 90 days. I was dumbfounded when the guide told me that after giving birth, the mother tigress would take the male cub away to some far-off places so that when he matures the chances of mating its mother or siblings are successfully precluded. Even among animals, incest is considered a taboo. Quite funny and queer are the ways of nature.

The sanctuary is also home to several other animals like lions, elephants, black monkeys (Nilgiri langur), Bagnoli deer, sambar deer, spotted deer, leopard, Indian gaur and many other animals and birds. We spotted many wild gaurs grazing in carefree delight. Our guide informed us that the gaurs spend the whole night in open grasslands huddled together to escape the prying eyes of the cunning tiger who hides among trees. Peacocks are common, a few of them with their marvelous bright colored tail feathers spread out which was a spectacular sight to behold. Many peahens were also seen around who were conspicuous by the absence of long, colorful plumes. Kaliyappan told us that the black monkeys are sharp observers and alert other animals about impending dangers. Due to this reason, they have the appellation, "sentinels of the forest". Kaliyappan was quite eloquent and my writing proficiency was no match for his fast-paced, unhindered narration. After a whirlwind visit and a few photo shoots of the dam site, we rushed to see the Kannimara teak, the oldest naturally grown teak tree in the world, which is a tourist attraction.

The Kannimara teak towered majestically above its fellow trees, its grandeur evoking the image of a medieval emperor reigning supreme over his loyal subjects.

The ancient tree is a native one of 450 years old and has a height of 38 meters and a girth of 7.5 meters. We were amazed by the sheer size and grandeur of the tree. Six of us stood in a circle, hand in hand, encompassing the tree's vast girth, our joined hands forming a human chain that encircled her sturdy trunk. Kaliyappan informed that all other teak trees were planted by the British and only Kannimara teak is a natural one. The lore has it that when the British tried to cut the tree down, it started bleeding much to the surprise of the local people and the British. So, they decided to spare the axe, giving the tree a new lease of life. In recognition of its age and gigantic size, which are a record of sorts, the government honored Kannimara teak by bestowing the "MAHAVRIKSHA" award in 1995. Kaliyappan concluded that the tree has an estimated value of ₹60-80 lakh. As nightfall descended and darkness started to envelope the forest, we started our return journey to Bison Valley.

The second day of the tour included a bamboo rafting in the Parambikkulam dam. The raft was manually driven by a trio headed by chief oarsman Manoharan. Like Kaliyappan, Manoharan too was quite articulate and enlightened us on the geographical peculiarities of the river. The forest is inhabited by the tribals and they protect the forest and its wealth with utmost respect and care. Manoharan said many fish species inhabit the dam but they never catch them as these fishes are the natural prey for hundreds of alligators that populate the dam. A rare example of man-animal cohabitation. Manoharan, Kaliyappan and their breed are dedicated Apostles of responsible tourism. The view from the raft was breathtakingly marvelous and the youngsters in our group exploited the opportunity to shoot photos of the captivating scenery.

We concluded our peregrination through the charming landscape after visiting the huge Parambikkulam-Aliyar dam and a couple of small dams and adjoining forest where we were warned by our guide that wild elephants and tigers would be roaming cheerfully. For me, the most fascinating thing about the forest is its deafening silence and serenity which we cannot experience anywhere else. The unearthly quietude was broken occasionally by the chirping of birds or the clatter of monkeys somewhere or the whooshing wind.

It was a wonderful journey that enriched my understanding of forests and enlightened my knowledge of wildlife. What saddened me most, however, was the complete absence of a natural forest. Our guide said that the once biodiversity-rich forest was plundered by the British imperial government, and replaced the rich and unique flora with teak trees. The replacement of native trees with a monoculture of teak has taken away much of the charm and beauty associated with a pristine forest. Thickets of Gin berry (*Paanal* in Malayalam) which is ubiquitous, is the only surviving species we could find in the teak plantation. The reserve is a haven not only for wildlife but also for the Indigenous tribes like the *Kadar* who contribute to the conservation efforts of the government.

21. *Chayakkada*: Kochi's Village Tea Shops

The cozy teashops of yore were a beehive of activities. Like elsewhere in Kerala, Kochi too was home to several village tea shops. These tea shops of varying types and sizes were once omnipresent in every nook and cranny of the village. Many were mere shacks with thatched roofs, and their walls and doors made of braided coconut fronds. Some refined versions were brick-walled and tile-roofed with wide front doors made of several wooden panes placed side by side in slots on thick wooden frames. These wide-open front doors covered the entire front facades of the shops.

Raghavan Chettan's *chayakkada* was one such tea shop in my village which was famed for tasty tea and delicious snacks. It was located by the side of Pullara Desam Road, a narrow, dusty village road of laterite. Raghavan Chettan was a short, fat man with thick silver-grey hair. He always wore a *kallimundu* which was folded above the knee and was bare chested revealing his stupendous pot belly. In those days menfolk of the village seldom wore shirts. The tea shop was housed in a small nondescript building with a tiled roof and wood-paned doors. There was a huge glass-fronted almirah with many shelves placed at a vantage place in the front. Passersby could easily get a full view of the various items displayed on the shelf. Items like *puttu* made of rice flour, *pazhampori, sukhiyan, bonda,* and *parippu vada* were the common foods available which were neatly arranged on the glass shelf. The stall was simply furnished with a couple of old wooden benches and tables and water collected in a tin container was kept outside with an old plastic mug, serving as the makeshift the handwashing station, where the customers could rinse their hands and mouths before enjoying the food. *Puttu* and *pappadam* or *puttu* and *kadalakkari* made a gorgeous blend and Raghavan Chettan's tea stall was renowned for this combo. Every time I walked past the tea stall, I would gaze longingly at the array of tantalizing finger foods on display, my desire for them bittersweet since my family never allowed bringing tea shop treats into our home.

Taking food from such outside eateries were then considered a low-class affair and Amma never encouraged us to take such foods though I carved for such munchies. However, whenever I visited Bhavani *Kunjamma*, my father's younger sister, who stayed nearby, she used to treat us with mouth-watering snacks from Raghavan Chettan's *chayakkada*. The snacks that I savored with such pleasure were what made my visits to *Kunjamma*'s house so enjoyable. In a corner of the shop, there was a large copper samovar kettle, the traditional urn. It's an appliance of Soviet origin which means "self-brewer". It was fired by coal from the bottom and it would be simmering with boiling water. I watched in wonder as he skillfully mixed the hot concoction, transferring it from one aluminum mug to another from great heights with precision. He then filtered it through a long, sagging cloth filter, called '*chaya pongi*' in local parlance, before dispensing the brew into glass tumblers. This unique way of mixing hot tea was then a common sight in Kerala. The making of the brew was an art in itself and the tea has earned the epithet "*meter chaya*" given the heights from where the hot beverage is transferred rapidly for mixing. The hot tea topped with a thick layer of froth was not just another beverage but an emotion.

There were quite a few regulars who would throng the shop for *chaya* and *kadi* and they would spend long hours there after finishing their food. The shop indeed was a meeting place that would awash village elders in the morning and evening where they would discuss threadbare sociopolitical issues. Occasions were not rare when these innocuous tit-tats would take violent forms leading to fisticuffs. This prompted Raghavan to put a warning notice in bold letters in Malayalam *"dayavucheyth evide raashtreeyam parayaruth"* which meant "please do not discuss politics here". Such warnings were displayed in many village teashops. The old Tamil songs flowing from the radio of nearby Premanandan's shop added to the soothing atmosphere.

In olden days, this kind of village tea shops were quite common in Kerala, frequented by tea aficionados and played a crucial role in spreading information in an era when social media was nonexistent and communications were slow and infrequent. The village tea shops were their favorite hangouts where they unburdened themselves with their pangs and pains after a day's hectic jobs. They discussed everything under the sun by sitting in the comforts of the stall, noisily sipping hot tea. The more knowledgeable and literate among them broke important news and events while the eloquent among them would steal the show with supplemental information. The news about man landing on the moon left them flabbergasted, while news about heinous crimes committed by Naxalites in north Kerala sent shockwave and unnerved them. They heard about the assassination of Mahatma Gandhi in utter disbelief, while the sudden demise of Nehru shell shocked them beyond words. These village tea shops were important milestones in the cultural milieu of the rural setting. It was a different world where a delightful blend of flavors, aromas, and cultural heritage was served.

22. Match Makers of Yesteryears

Today marriages right from matchmaking to the final ritual of tying the knots and the subsequent lavish spread of delicious foods have all gone hi-tech and professional which the matrimonial agencies and event management team conduct.

In my childhood days, marriage brokers played a significant role in facilitating marriages. This particular class of people, who were engaged as marriage brokers, were commonly referred to as *vivaha dallal* which meant a marriage broker. True to their name, they acted as third-party intermediaries negotiating on behalf of the brides' and grooms' sides between them based on social status, wealth, and family connections. As marriage brokers, they played a catalytic role in bringing together two different families from different social backgrounds and, as such, enjoyed wide respect and hospitality. Both men and women were engaged in this profession, some full-time and others moonlighted. Some of them had a good knowledge of astrology which helped them to earn good clientship. Because among the Hindus, the laborious task of matchmaking always began with matching the horoscope, which along with caste and class mattered more than anything else. They would be omnipresent in all functions and festivities of the small town. Temples, churches, and such social spaces were their favored hangouts. In these locations, they looked out for boys and girls of marriageable ages and once such youngsters are spotted, they would approach the parents of the prospective groom/bride with alliances from suitable boy/girl. In those days the male brokers could be easily made out by the way they dressed and spoke. As a rule, all of them were attired in white spotless *mundu* and white shirts with a large pocket in which they kept a pen and leather-bound diary in the armpit which contained the contact details of many prospective grooms and brides and a *kaalan kuda*, an umbrella with curved handle. Many had a distinct sandalwood paste mark, *chandana kuri*, on the forehead.

If either the groom or the bride had *chowa dosham*, which happens due to the inauspicious placing of Mars in the horoscope, this provided an opportunity to the brokers. This was interpreted as ineffable miseries and misfortune including untimely death of the partner for the one who had *chowa dosham*. Only solution was to find a partner with similar *chowa dosham* and marry. Girls with *chowa dosham* was always a good fortune for the brokers as they could demand a hefty amount as commission from the girls' parents apart from the normal ones from the grooms' parents.

The preliminary stages of matchmaking process would begin with sharing photos and *rasi chakra*, the zodiac of the prospective girls and boys. If the horoscopes are matching the process would progress into successive steps like *"pennukanal"* which means "seeing the girls". A small group comprising the groom along with elders like the boy's parents, uncles, and aunts accompanied by the broker would make a short visit which would be announced well in advance for the bride's family to plan. The women in the group are specifically trained to evaluate the feminine assets of the girl. In those days it was common for the elder women from the groom's side to ask the girl to lift the bottom of her skirt to ascertain that the bride was free from filariasis. Till the late seventies filariasis was a serious health issue among Keralites, especially in Alappuzha region. It was with the objective of the eradication of such diseases that the government established a unit of Vector Control Research Centre (VCRC) under Indian Council of Medical Research (ICMR) at Cherthala in Alappuzha.

Chellappan whom we affectionately addressed as Chellappan Chettan was a marriage broker of good standing in the early seventies. It was through his mediation that an acceptable proposal was finally materialized for my second sister. Since she had "issues" with her zodiac, perfect matchmaking proved an elusive task. Chellappan himself brought proposals from many prospective grooms but failed to match the horoscope of my sister. But for a broker, it's immaterial as he charged for each visit some small amount towards his travelling and sundry expenses which Amma used to pay albeit reluctantly. And finally, after a prolonged search and several rounds of unsuccessful *"pennukanal"*, a suitable proposal was brought up by Chellappan much to the relief of everyone in our family. Then the subsequent process like customary visits by the elders of the girl's family which was reciprocated by the boy's family leading to the engagement were all completed in a short time. Unlike today's engagement ceremonies marked by extravagant celebrations, in the olden days it was a simple affair in which only the closest relatives of both the groom and bride numbering a dozen or so participated. The ritual included the exchange of the horoscope, written usually on a palm leaf, between the *Ammavan* of the boy and girl followed by a traditional *sadya* which would be a sumptuous vegetarian lunch with an array of curries, *pappadam*, p*azham*, and *payasam*. A mutually acceptable date and time of marriage would be fixed on this occasion. In the past, neither the groom nor the bride possessed the freedom to choose their own partner, instead, all decisions regarding the match were made by the parents and other senior family members. Amma often recounted that upon her departure from her home Pullyadath to Thaiveettil after her marriage, she was engulfed by a profound sense of estrangement. The thought of leaving behind the home of her childhood and youth, a place animated by the laughter and presence of her siblings, and the watchful eyes of her caring parents, was beyond her imagination. The friends in her neighborhood, once a source of joy and camaraderie, now seemed distant memories. The home she cherished as her own had, in an instant, turned unfamiliar. As she stepped into her husband's residence, she felt like a fish out of water. Such is the harsh reality of our patriarchal society, where the emotional trauma following marriage is a burden silently borne by many Indian women.

With the fulfillment of the marriage, the responsibilities of the marriage broker ended, and he was paid a good amount as commission by the boy's father which depended on the dowry and ornaments which the bride brought along. Similarly, the girl's parents would also give an equally impressive amount depending on the profession, social status, and financial soundness of the groom. Their influence left an indelible mark on the institution of marriage. With computerization and the growth of matrimonial agencies the traditional marriage brokers have become a rare breed which will soon become extinct.

23. Free Ranging Village Dogs

In our good old days, almost every household had one or two native dogs. They thrived on the meager food which the families shared and on the offal of fish and meat. They were very loving and caring dogs who roamed freely in the locality. They only barked and seldom bit as the adage says. They barked only at strangers and wagged their tails whenever a familiar figure entered the courtyard, whether regulars like newspaper boys and postmen or occasional visitors like fish or vegetable vendors. However, if anyone trespasses into the neighborhood, the entire dogs of the locality would unite to confront him ferociously, until the intruder makes a retreat.

During my boyhood days, we had a deeply affectionate and loving dog. His name was Watcher and true to his name he proved himself a real watchdog and our homestead was under his surveillance. He had two neighborhood friends, Stalin and Emden. During the daytime, the trio would wander around the locality but by evening they would return to their respective homes. Watcher used to accompany Amma when she paid visits to nearby temples and the houses of relatives. One rainy evening Watcher breathed his last at a ripe old age of 15. Incidentally, this happened the night before the *Karkidaka Vavu*, a significant

Hindu ritual observed in Kerala to honor deceased ancestors, and we were busily preparing for the ritualistic *daham vekkal.* Amma said that it's good that he departed on an auspicious day as if to console us.

In those days the villagers used to name their pet dogs after famous people without ever understanding the significance of those names. Celebrity names like Emden, Stalin, Tipu, Kaiser, Jimmy, Tarzan, Pinto and Tojo were quite popular for dogs. They led a happy, peaceful, and independent life. They were allowed to roam and breed freely by their owners. They were the sentinels of the village. Back then the owners were quite ignorant of pedigrees. No one ever bothered about the breed of his or her dog nor anyone asked for it. A dog was just a dog, nothing more. They used to pee and poop freely as and when they wanted. They had the liberty to socialize with themselves and with humans. In short, they peacefully coexisted with humans and also with other animals like goats, cats, and chickens. However, a few affluent people in the village had exotic breeds like Pomeranian, Alsatian, and Doberman which were either kenneled or leashed.

There is a newfound love, particularly among the urban elite to own and foster dogs of exotic breeds. This growing preference for such foreign breeds proved detrimental to the survival of our native dogs. Compared to the foreign breeds, the native species are more friendly, loyal, loving, disease resistant, and are accustomed to the local climates.

One does not understand how "man's best friend" was turned all on a sudden into the worst foe ever. Many Indian cities are already in the grip of continuing stray dog attacks as the citizenry in such places lives under the constant fear of dog bites. The series of onslaughts by street dogs has caused popular protests and much consternation to the government.

The opinions are divided on the issue with a section of the population strongly urging the government to end the threat by mass killings while the animal lovers are vehemently opposed to such drastic measures. According to these animal enthusiasts, the man's best friends, who dwell on the streets deserve a better deal from the civil society and the government. The Delhi High Court in a recent judgment has echoed similar sentiments and it underscored the need for feeding and caring for these friendly animals by residence associations. Homeward migration necessitated by Covid-19 has forced many migrants to abandon their pet dogs. Months of neglect by their caregivers and hunger precipitated by the pandemic-enforced isolation have made the once-friendly native dogs our arch enemies.

Packs of native dogs have well-defined territorial jurisdiction of their own and seldom venture beyond their limits. These native dogs are harmless and thrive on foods provided by the neighborhood residents. The main reason for the sudden spurt in the population of stray dogs is the carelessly abandoned food surpluses and slaughterhouse wastes.

To combat the stray dog menace, measures can be taken, including: humane trapping, sterilization, and release; public education on responsible pet ownership and stray dog issues; improving waste management to reduce attractants; and enforcing animal welfare laws to prevent cruelty and neglect.

24. Amma and Her Reading Sessions

Though Amma had only primary education she had a penchant for reading and had an inquisitive and sharp mind. She used to read *Mathrubhumi* every day. She followed a strict daily routine. Every morning, she would rise early and devote several hours to household tasks. Following lunch, she would take a brief nap, a habitual practice. Afterwards, she would dedicate time to reading, a cherished part of her daily schedule. In those days ours was the only house in the locality to subscribe to newspapers. Women of the locality numbering a few would gather in the veranda of our old house where they would huddle together. They would engage in gossip where they discussed every conceivable thing. In their midst, Amma would keep her *thambalam*, neatly arranged with an array of vital ingredients for chewing such as betel leaves, arecanut sliced into very small pieces, *pokala* (dried tobacco), and a paste of lime in a *noottukudam*, which is a small oblong shaped brass container with a flat base and a small opening on top with a conical lid. Many of the younger generations would not have seen a *vettila thambalam* and may not know what it looks like. It's a thick, circular brass plate with a small circular compartment projecting in the middle of the tray with three small legs for support. It's inside the middle cup that the small arecanut pieces were kept. The paraphernalia also includes a spittoon (*kolamby*) made of brass to spit out. I vividly remember elder women from our neighborhood like Thresia Chechi, Padmakshy Chechi, Dakshayani Chechi, Thankamma Chechi, and a few other women who would gather in our house in the afternoon. They used to discuss a host of subjects many of which were alien to me. But I remember that whenever an important event had taken place, these women would request Amma to read the news for them as all of them were illiterates. She would oblige them and read the news loud and clear. When Amma read, every one listened. I vividly recall the day in July 1969 when the news of the first manned moon landing was shared with them. The announcement was met with disbelief, and the accompanying photographs in the newspaper left them in awe. There was all-round disbelief, and in unison, they questioned the veracity. Amma explained to them the historic event in detail, leavened with her version of the story. I don't know whether she herself believed the news. However, she vehemently brushed aside all their doubts claiming that what appears in the newspaper is 100% true and no need to cast aspersions on their authenticity. This seemed to satisfy the other women in the group to some extent regarding the genuineness of the news. In between the reading-cum- gossip sessions, she would serve her compatriots mouthful shares of betel nuts and leaves. She kept the *thambalam* like an *akshayapatra* with frequent refilling of chewing ingredients.

Another occasion when these neighborhood women compelled Amma to read the news aloud for them was during the Naxalite attacks in Wayanad involving the Pulppally police station attack. The frontline Naxalite leaders of the day like Kunnickal Narayanan, his wife Mandakini, and daughter Ajita all came alive in their imagination, invoking fear and awe in them, thanks to Amma's incredible reading ability.

Amma's readings once again held her friends spellbound when she discussed the notorious Mariyakkutty murder case. This high-profile crime, which rocked the state, involved a priest's complicity in the brutal killing of Mariyakkutty, leaving the public stunned and horrified.

Later a couple of films were made based on this real incident like *Mainatharuvi* and *Madatharuvi*. Amma thoroughly enjoyed the company of these women and together they celebrated their little pleasures in life. Back then though these women from the neighborhood lived in abject poverty; they enjoyed life. Condemned to live in a virtual world controlled by AI and enhanced by AR, we will never fully appreciate the authentic connections and friendships that existed in the past, unbridled by the constraints of social hierarchy, religion, and background.

After Achan's retirement, this afternoon gatherings of women became infrequent as he never encouraged such gatherings. Gradually Amma's *ayalpakka koottayma*, the neighborhood gathering, where everyone enjoyed the relaxed atmosphere and bonhomie, became a thing of the past. Bowing to Achan's dictum Amma gave up her betel chewing habit too. She taught me lessons of empathy, kindness, and compassion. I still cherish her love, guidance, and unwavering presence.

25. Minimalism as a Way of Village Life

Gone are the days when we led a life of minimalism characterized by limited needs. We used to visit the nearby shops with a set list in which only the most essential items figured. Amma never encouraged us to buy anything out of this list. Whenever the stock of grocery items was exhausted, she would send my elder sister to the grocery store of Parameswaran Chetan in the village market where he supplied all items on credit. Once Amma received the Money Order that Achan would send at the beginning of the month, the first thing she did was to settle the accounts of the grocery store. Buying new clothes for Onam was considered a luxury. Our needs were meager and we made the fullest use of every item we purchased. We had a minimum set of clothes, and a pair of footwear, household items would be limited to the bare minimum. Unknowingly we were practicing minimalism.

In sharp contrast, we lead a life of profligacy being fanned by consumerism. We tend to buy articles that we either do not need or are not of immediate use. Credit cards give us a false sense of financial security and we end up spending beyond our means. We no longer visit a supermarket or shopping mall with a prepared list prioritizing our needs. Recently addressing a gathering dominated by children and young adults, noted writer and philanthropist Sudha Murthy exhorted them to follow a simple life marked by minimalism. Ms. Murthy, being herself an ardent follower of minimalism in her life and thoughts, is well within her rights to advise Gen X.

In recent years minimalism has become a new mantra, which has been oft quoted in and out of place. Minimalism is a concept that is gaining much currency in developed nations as a way of life that would unburden the practitioner from unnecessary baggage in life and eventually lead to a more peaceful and contended life. It's all about making intelligent choices about what is to be kept and what is to be eliminated. De-cluttering is the cornerstone of minimalism and it involves getting rid of unwanted things. In many houses bed rooms are the most cluttered place with every unwanted thing being abandoned. Such bedrooms, no doubt, would distract the occupants and would impair their sleeping habits. Go instead for minimalist bedrooms with minimalist wardrobes. In many modern apartments and households, toys occupy a significant portion of living space. De-clutter them either by eliminating the ones no longer used or gifting them to orphanages for destitute children.

This concept can be practiced by anyone by modifying their lifestyle, changing mindset, and cutting down on unwanted possessions and comforts. It's all about satisfying our needs rather than our greed which is the attribute of consumerism. It involves identifying the necessary in your life and avoiding the rest which means that we buy items that are necessary. Before buying anything, we should ask ourselves whether the particular item is necessary, and if the answer is YES, we can go ahead with the particular purchase. Otherwise, we can postpone it to sometime in the future like clothing, decor, hobbies, and objects of snob appeals. Minimalism enables many perceptible advantages to its followers like more economical use of money and other resources, de-cluttering of living space, a significant reduction in waste generation, decreased use of water and energy, a more environmental way of life, and above all the satisfaction of leading an eco-friendly life. Fewer possessions lead to fewer distractions and more happiness in your home. Use a minimum amount of furniture and wherever possible use convertible types or multipurpose ones like sofa cum bed or diwan's cot. Another area that is cluttered in most houses is the kitchen which is used as a convenient space to dump all and sundry. A cluttered kitchen dispersed with unwanted things is a common sight in most Indian houses. Buy only the essential food items and that too locally available fruits and vegetables because food articles sourced from far away locations generate large amounts of carbon dioxide during transportation. Focus on essentials and avoid trivial. As far as possible modify food habits by including plentiful fruits and vegetables as they can be eaten raw or with minimum cooking which reduces the emission of greenhouse gases. The aim should be to optimize resources and make a nutrient-dense food that has minimum impact on the environment.

Academics, researchers, and voracious readers can replace printed books with digital versions. Apart from saving space, would obviate the need for occasional disposal of yellowish, moth-eaten, and dust-covered old books and periodicals. This also reduces the pressures on forest wealth with decreased use of paper. Try to purchase products that are durable, reusable, and have prolonged life. Minimize dependence on single-use items like paper glasses and plates, tissue, and cutlery. During long travels, it's a sensible idea to carry a set of plates, glass, spoons, and cutlery of our own and to reduce reliance on disposable items which have huge pollution potential. Encourage students and youngsters to write using a fountain pen or a ballpoint pen that can be refilled and used for many years instead of use-and-throw type inexpensive pen.

In the olden days, we used to visit grocery stores with a list of essentials to be purchased. In modern days, we visit shopping malls and supermarkets and indulge in purchases most of them non-essential articles. To attract such naive customers the supermarkets often arrange branded items in a very attractive and appealing manner with mind-boggling color lights, very often with discounts and credit facilities, a system referred to as "visual merchandising" in managerial parlance. The lure is so irresistible that many fall into the trap and end up purchasing unwanted items. Consumerism has been so entrenched in our lives that visits to the nearby malls have become a part of our weekend agenda.

Ecocentrism was embedded in the old village life where we relied on natural materials for everyday needs. We used leaves of Colocasia and plantain to wrap most food items like meat and fish while old newspaper for fruits and vegetables. Groceries were wrapped in paper bags, and we used cloth bags to carry everything.

Minimalist living involves de-cluttering, organizing, and minimizing intentionally so that life becomes simpler and more pleasurable. Cut on luxurious spending, refrain from being a spendthrift. Follow a "penny wise pound foolish" approach in money matters. From a holistic point of view divest yourself of unwanted objects, practices, thoughts, memories and you will be able to experience the benefits of minimalism. Practice Minimalism as a way of life and is going to pay its dividends.

26. Driven By Wheels: My Automotive Obsessions

Just like any other village boy of the bygone decades I too had a strong affection for motor cars which were a rarity back then. Ambassador and Fiat dominated the automotive market, they ruled the roost. My preferred car was an Ambassador. Only very few and the very rich could afford exciting cars like Morri's Minor, Chevrolets, Benz, and Impala. Expensive Indian-made cars like Contessa came to the market only much later. In our locality only three people owned cars, an Ambassador owned by Sudarsan, the Regional Manager of Nestle, a Fiat owned by Kalarickal Gopalakrishnan, who had an agency of Murphy and Philips radios and a Fiat owned by Kochanchery Gopalan who was a wealthy businessman and a social worker. I was distantly related to all three aristocratic families through Amma and whenever she visited their families, I always accompanied her for the sheer joy and excitement of watching and touching those cars parked in the garage. Once I traveled along with Amma in the Fiat of Kochanchery Gopalan as co travelers along with his wife to attend a relative's marriage in a nearby small town. In my village a couple of taxi cars were available and for all emergencies and celebrations, the villagers depended on them.

The first vehicle I ever owned in life was an old worn-out cycle tyre that I procured from my friend Xavier, our neighbor Mariya Kutty's son, for twenty paise. There existed an enormous bonhomie between us. At the time, I was in the fifth grade and most of my friends owned such "vehicles" in which they "travelled" through village alleys in the evening. One day Xavier told me that he was planning to sell a cycle tyre from his prized collection. Considering my close friendship, he agreed to give the tyre at a discounted price. It was indeed an exhilarating offer that I could not ignore. So, I started collecting money and from the *vishukaineettam*, a part was set apart towards the purchase of the pre-owned "vehicle". Finally, when enough money was collected, I approached Xavier and purchased my dream vehicle. He was benevolent enough to give me the best out of his worst collection of discarded cycle tyres. I was ecstatic and for me, it was a dream come true. A value-for-money purchase indeed, I told myself. I kept my purchase of the treasured asset a closely guarded secret and kept it behind the cow shed away from the prying eyes of my elder sister.

From the next day onwards, I too joined the "elite" class of village children who owned such cycle tyres. We navigated through the narrow and winding village alleys lined by thickets of wild growth. I thoroughly enjoyed my evenings after school in the company of other tyre drivers.

However, a few of us had upgraded to metal bicycle rims. Initially, I was thrilled with my new vehicle, but the excitement wore off after a few days of riding. The vehicle lost its appeal, and I grew tired of the tyres. I longed to upgrade to metal rims like my friends Henry and Joy, who had gleaming metal rims that sparked envy and admiration among the rest of us.

I confided my desire with Xavier and he suggested exchanging my cycle tyre with a bicycle rim for which I had to pay an additional premium of fifty paise. At the end of prolonged negotiations, he agreed to exchange for forty paise. From the balance of the *vishukaineettam*, which was earmarked for buying old textbooks for the next academic year from my senior Francis, forty paise was thus paid to Xavier and this time I became the arrogant owner of a bicycle rim.

When I came home with the bicycle rim my sister happened to see the purchase and the matter was promptly reported to Amma. Amma became suspicious and looked at me with a quizzical expression. I was quizzed thoroughly to know about the source of the money and when the truth was revealed she had sent me back to Xavier to return the rim and get the money back. The reason for her decision to return the bicycle rim had nothing to do with my diversion of money but because she was concerned about my health, as ever since I became the owner of the cycle tyre and started driving it, my cough and breathing troubles, which were recurring, worsened. My second brother-in-law, who happened to be there, also vehemently opposed the prospect of myself running after the bicycle rim. All this opposition to my ambitious dream had come as fly in the ointment. Finally, with a sense of reluctance, I returned the rim to Xavier and explained my predicament. Without any hesitation, he took back the rim and returned my money instantly. My dream of a vehicle of my own thus came to an abrupt end.

Thirty years later, I finally had the opportunity to own a vehicle again. I bought a pre-owned white Maruti Omni from a lawyer for Rs 1.25 lakh in 1999.

The car boasted a distinctive number plate: KL06/5151. The next day, we held a blessing ceremony for the vehicle at the nearby Sree Bhavaneeswara Temple, followed by a special *Vahana Pooja* ritual at Kottarakkara Maha Ganapathi Temple.

The problem erupted as I had neither the skill nor the confidence to drive the car and eventually, though reluctantly I appointed a driver. The young driver's skill was worse than mine but his confidence was double than what I had. Moreover, I had to adjust my travelling needs according to his whims and fancies. This had annoyed Achan and he arranged a special driving class session exclusively for me in a nearby driving school for which he paid a fat amount as a fee. It was this gesture of Achan that later instilled confidence in me and enabled me to self-drive with confidence.

Right from the start, the car was plagued with persistent problems. Achan recommended selling the aging vehicle and upgrading to a brand-new model.

This is how I upgraded from the old Omni to a red brand-new Hyundai Santro, for which Achan gave his modest contribution. A few years later, the car was upgraded to a silver Maruti Swift, after another few years a greenish brown Honda Amaze, and finally to an auto transmission white Hyundai Creta, the one I have been using for the past few years. I drove my first car when I was thirty-nine. During my adolescence, I never thought, even in my wildest dreams, that I would one day own a modern, new-generation car and drive it myself. It was beyond the imagination of a village boy like me. The journey from a village boy rolling a worn-out cycle tyre to a sixty-three-year-old driving a modern car equipped with the latest digital technologies is truly amazing

In my childhood days I used to tell Amma that when I grow up, I would buy an Ambassador and take her around in the car. At that time, a car was beyond the imagination of a middle-class boy. But later in life, when I bought a car of my own, she was too weak and too old to travel. However, she relished the sight of her beloved son owning and driving a car, quite oblivious to the days when I 'drove' cycle tyre.

27. Kerala's Water Wells: A Source of Life and Culture

In the distant past wells were a ubiquitous source of drinking water in many parts of Kerala. Public wells were then a common sight in many areas including schools, hospitals, markets, and colonies where poor people dwelled and these public utilities were built and maintained by panchayats. Till recently, there was a public well in Palluruthy Veli which was used by the merchants in the market. The laterite stone built well was equipped with a pulley which was supported by a frame of concrete. The six-month-long monsoon replenished the water perpetually, guaranteeing a year-round supply of plentiful water. Even during the hot summer months, these wells contained water. Traditionally, expert artisans honed their skills in constructing wells with brick masonry, developing innovative rainwater harvesting systems that optimized water collection and storage. These wells served as a bounty of fresh water, providing a reliable source for the community. To ensure water quality, wells were strategically dug in areas far removed from septic tanks and toilets, preventing contamination and maintaining the water's purity. In days of old, a ring made from the dense, inner heartwood of the gooseberry tree (*nellipalaka*) was used to line the bottom of wells. This natural filter was thought to impart a sweet flavor to the already crystal-clear water

Wells are an indispensable part of Kerala temples and for every temple, irrespective of its size, a well containing clean and pure water is a necessity that is used for all auspicious purposes like bathing the deity, cleaning the temple premises, and even preparing *nivedyam*. Such temple wells are well protected and only the priests are allowed to use them. As a rule, it would be inside the temple close to the *Sreekovil*, the sanctum sanctorum.

During my childhood days in the early sixties, a few households in the area had wells that ensured plentiful water which lasted throughout the year. In old *tharavad* such wells were common and were located alongside the kitchen so that water could be drawn from inside the kitchen using buckets attached to coir ropes. Wooden, drum-shaped pulleys were employed to make the task of drawing water. Until the mid-1970s, when piped drinking water became widely available, wells remained a steadfast and reliable source of fresh water in Kerala, providing a dependable supply for the community

In my house we had a well that was excavated in the late sixties, till then we depended on a hand pump for our needs of water. It was made of prefabricated concrete rings which are stacked one above the other. Even today it remains the sole source of water for the entire household, except for cooking and drinking, for which we depend on municipal water.

Keeping in tune with the changing times, we replaced the old buckets and installed a submersible pump instead, with pipe connections and water taps wherever they are needed. When our old house underwent renovation two decades ago, the well was incorporated into the garage, posing a challenge for parking vehicles. Consequently, many people suggested that we fill in the well, as it was hindering vehicle access and causing inconvenience. But despite the inconvenience, we still keep the well, properly maintained in the front yard, for we know very well that there is no substitute for the clean and pristine perennial source of water.

28. The Mysterious Disappearance of M.V. Kairali: "The Titanic of Kerala"

July-15, 1979, Kerala woke up to the alarming news about the mysterious disappearance of M V Kairali along with her 49 crew and 20,538 tons iron ore which she was carrying. Back then I was undergoing my Pre Degree course at Cochin College. The news shocked everyone and for the subsequent few weeks, Newspapers were filled with fanciful stories about the mishap. The disaster became the talking point wherever people gathered. Many naval experts likened this to the tragedy that struck Titanic and described Kairali as "The Titanic of Kerala".

Naval history is abounded with innumerable stories of shipwrecks and capsizing of ships mid-sea, many of which are mysterious and beyond explanation. Even now the tragedy that struck "Titanic" over a century ago is a painful saga, the memories of which are still haunting human sensibilities, even though the wreck has been recovered and the reasons for the tragedy are established beyond any doubt.

M V Kairali was the sole ship owned by the Kerala Shipping Corporation, a full government-owned shipping company. A bulk carrier "Oscarsord" built in Norway in 1996, she was purchased by KSC two years later from her original owner for ₹ 5.81 crores and she was rechristened as "M V Kairali".

On 30th June 1979, she was on a routine cruise, this time carrying 20,538 tons of iron ore from Margao, in Goa to Rostock, Germany via Djibouti where she was scheduled for refueling. It was a wet monsoon day and for many days it has been raining heavily. When she left, she had 49 crew onboard apart from the voluminous cargo that she was carrying. In those days navigation and communication with land-based control centers were not well developed. The only means of communication were the radio telephone and radar, the dependable navigational tool. The last message from the vessel was received by Bombay Radio, the official agency for communication with the ship, was on 3rd July. As the ship failed to reach Djibouti on 8th July, its local agent contacted KSC after three days and informed that the whereabouts of the vessel were untraceable. This has sent a shockwave through the state and a shell-shocked KSC started search operations with the help of the Navy and Coast Guard. The government appeared completely nonplussed. However, the prolonged searches proved futile as she vanished mysteriously into the depths of the ocean without leaving any trace. The newspapers then carried detailed stories many of which were mere gossip and unfounded reports. But one thing is true, the apathy of the concerned authorities and the unpardonable delay in ordering the search operations.

There were unconfirmed reports of the malfunctioning of the radar on the fateful sail and also the allegation that the captain was pressured to load more cargo than its allowed quantity.

Several theories have been put forth as possible causes for the sudden disappearance of the vessel which included the vessel being forcibly taken by Somalian pirates and resorted to shipbreaking after abandoning the crew in some uninhibited islands. Another theory is that the overloaded vessel suddenly capsized without leaving time to leave even an SOS message as the sea was quite rough during the monsoon season. This theory has some substance as iron ore fines tends to liquify when it comes into contact with moisture and can risk the safety and stability of the ship. As the ship was insured for ₹6 crores, which KSC has received as a claim, there were allegations that the disappearance of the ship was a well-planned ploy to garner the insurance. Nevertheless, all these theories are not strong enough to reinforce the fact that a huge bulk carrier has suddenly sunk into the depths of the ocean in a split second. Her sudden disappearance along with her crew and cargo remains an enduring maritime mystery leaving many unanswered questions. Even today her disappearance into the depths of the Indian Ocean remains an unexplained and unresolved mystery wrapped in an enigma perhaps as a stark reminder of the impermanence and fragility of human existence

Noted Malayalam filmmaker Jude Anthony has to make an investigative thriller on celluloid based on the true story of the mysterious disappearance of Kairali.

29. Sanchayika: Piggy Banks to Passbooks; A History of Student Savings in Yesteryears

Ours is a generation that had few opportunities to handle money during our childhood years, unlike today. Our parents and elders in the family never encouraged us to handle money as matters related to money transactions were all the privileges enjoyed only by the grown-ups in the family.

During my childhood years in the mid-sixties and early seventies, we were allowed to transact only in coins of smaller denominations and that too only under unavoidable circumstances. Back then coins were available in denominations of 1,2,3,5,10,20,25 and 50 paise. Coins 25 and 50 were commonly referred to as 4 Ana and 8 Ana respectively (one Ana was approximately equal to six paise).

As his remuneration for his selfless work, Unni *Aasaan* would be paid a modest amount of 25 paise as *dakshina* on every Saturday. While handing over the fee every week Amma would constantly remind me to take care of the quarter Ana coin as in those days it was a big sum for her. Thus, I enjoyed the opportunity to handle money and gently caressed the coin before being offered to *Aasaan*. I remember in the mid-sixties Amma used to purchase rice for 25 paise a Kg, tapioca for 10 paise a kg, and salt for 2 paise a kg from the nearby small grocery shop of Vypisserry Manuel.

When I was in high school, the central government launched a savings bank scheme for school children, which thrilled the students. This initiative, designed to instill a savings habit in young minds, was conceived by the visionary leader, Mrs. Indira Gandhi

Started in early 1970, the scheme encouraged students to start a savings habit at a very early age and taught the functioning of the bank realistically. Sanchayika was the name of the scheme. It was introduced in our school at the behest of T.P. Peethambaran Master, our Head Master, who was an erudite teacher and an honest politician who later became a senior political leader at the national level. In those days campus politics often took an ugly turn and violent agitations by student organizations were common. During those tumultuous years, Master struggled to reinstate peace on the campus by bringing the warring groups together. Back then he was a close confidant and party colleague of Mrs. Indira Gandhi. Master represented the Palluruthy Assembly Constituency thrice in the Kerala Assembly spanning eleven years. He was a vocal proponent of value-based politics which he practiced in his political career stretching eight decades. The Sanchayika scheme was operated by Kumara Pillai Master, our class teacher, and the bank functioned every Friday from 1.30 to 2.00 pm.

It was a dream come true for us to operate a savings bank account in our name and was quite a thrilling experience for us. We had the liberty to deposit any amount from 10 paise. When I informed Amma about Sanchayika she allowed me to join the scheme though hesitantly.

On one Friday, I joined Sanchayika by opening an account and making an initial deposit of 25 paise. A few days later Kumara Pillai Master provided all account holders with a small pocket-sized passbook which was blue colored with a blurred image of a few school children. Just like any bank passbook, the Sanchayika passbook too had details like remittances and withdrawals. Being gifted with such a passbook further encouraged us to deposit in our accounts. Every Friday Amma used to give me an amount varying from 20 to 25 paise. Additionally, I began saving a portion of my pocket money, which Amma gave me for errands like buying cattle feed and groceries. By cutting back on unnecessary expenses like buying toffees, I was able to increase my weekly deposits into Sanchayika.

As per the rules the account has to be closed when the student leaves his/her school. When we completed our SSLC, just before the commencement of the study leave, one afternoon our "banker teacher" announced that our Sanchayika account would be closed the coming Friday. After three years of savings, we were elated by the thought that we would receive a handsome amount and we fancied how we spend the money. My savings totaled ₹26.75 while the richest among us had a whooping ₹75.00. I handed over my entire amount to Achan from which he gave me enough money to take a membership in the neighborhood library, Sanmargodayam Library & Reading Room.

The Sanchayika scheme which was started in June 1970, was popular in Kerala and played a major role in popularizing and encouraging the habit of savings among school children. However, the scheme was discontinued in October, 2016 for some reasons. In this age of spending sprees, often beyond one's means, by using credit cards, a scheme like Sanchayika will help to instill a habit of frugality and thriftiness by using money wisely. Frugality and simplicity are two finer aspects of life that we need to inculcate in our younger generations.

30. The Revenge of Chandrabhanu and The Great Fire of Cochin.

Anyone who has visited Fort Kochi beach in recent decades might have noticed a tall and slender stone pillar, planted alongside the beach behind the Bastian Bungalow, left to the vagaries of nature and being disfigured with graffiti and posters. If you happened to behold this mighty pillar, you are looking at an ancient artifact of immense historic significance, a silent reminder of an inferno that had swept through the city 135 years ago.

It was in 1795 that the British conquered Fort Cochin and after the conquest, the city came to be known as British Cochin. Back then Cochin had a legacy of building magnificent ships in teak wood and she had the technical expertise and human capital necessary for shipbuilding. Initially, the British underestimated the capabilities of the local people in building ships but later realized that they had extraordinary skill and creativity in shipbuilding which made them jealous. Soon the imperial government made rules that banned the Indians from building ships. Instead, the British constructed their shipyards in and around Cochin. The historic Brunton & Company shipyard, a British-owned enterprise, was formerly located at the site now occupied by the entrance of the new Thoppumpady Bridge, serving as a reminder of the area's significant shipbuilding heritage.

Disregarding the British dictum, a native naval architect made one ship much to the embarrassment of his British babus. The British court denied permission for the ship to sail in Indian waters. However, the courageous man who made the ship decided to operate it ignoring the British order. On the fateful day of 4th January 1889; the 500-tonne ship, named "Chandrabhanu", was readied for its maiden voyage. The ship had been loaded with tons of coconut oil, coconut fiber (*chakiri*), coir, carpets, and spices. This angered the British authorities and they ordered to impound the ship which was then tied up in the river mouth at Kamaala Kadavu, close by the Volkart Bros, a British company engaged in the export of coconut oil and fibers. But being exposed to extreme heat and sunlight, a fire broke out on the upper deck of the ship which was sheltered by coconut fronds. The British officials noticed the fire but did nothing to extinguish it, instead, ordered their carpenters to snap the coir ropes tethered to the ship and set her free. No sooner than later the entire ship was engulfed by flames. What happened thereafter was something weird, uncanny. The untethered ship on fire had moved forward by the strong sea wind. The burning Chandrabhanu moved menacingly forward as if in revenge and setting fire to all the huge British godowns including Volkart Bros, Aspinwall & Co, Brunton Boatyard, and Pierce Leslie which were located along the Fort Cochin Barmouth from Kamaala Kadavu to Calvetty. The fire also destroyed more than 300 houses in the locality and finally, Chandrabhanu sunk into the depths of Fort Cochin backwaters as a huge fireball. Historian K.L. Bernard gives a detailed account of the shocking incident in his book "Flashes of Kerala History" under the chapter "Great Fire of Cochin".

The new generation of the city is quite oblivious of this sordid chapter in the history of Fort Cochin and the only reminder is the stone pillar. The inscription on the stone pillar reads, "Erected October 1890 by J.E. Winkler, Port Officer, the great fire of Cochin, 4th January 1889". Today the stone pillar is the only surviving memorial of the great fire.

Its high time the Archaeological Survey of India (ASI) or Indian National Trust for Art and Cultural Heritage (INTACH) took measures to protect the stone pillar by preserving it in a museum as a protected monument for posterity.

31. The Village Library and the Fascinating World of Book

As a teenager, I profoundly enjoyed the sweet, fruity aroma that emanated from the pages of new books. Whenever a new book was purchased, I would smell it many times and savor the sweet fragrance before I read it. New books are not only to be read but also to be savored by scent-such is the unwritten rule of bibliophiles. It was Dr. Oliver Tearle, an English professor in the UK who coined a term to describe the love for the smell of books, the word is *"bibliosmia"* derived from the Greek words *biblion* (meaning book) and *osme* (meaning scent, smell or odor). I'm indeed a *bibliophile* with an intense sense of *bibliosmia*.

I was encouraged to read fiction by Sivan Chettan, my neighbor, who was a voracious reader. He used to share his library books with my two elder sisters who were also interested in reading and occasionally I would scan through them for the mere pleasure of enjoying the smell of old books. He was a great inspiration for me to foray into the world of books and suggested I too take a membership in the library. It was in the mid-seventies that I became a member of Sanmargodayam Library & Reading Room, the village library at Palluruthy. A small, tiled building by the side of Pullara Desam Road, housed the library which had a small yet wonderful collection of Malayalam books, mostly novels. The building was partitioned into two unequal rooms, while the smaller room functioned as a library the larger one was the reading room. In the reading room, half a dozen wooden benches and desks were kept while the library had a few wooden almirahs stuffed with books. The village elders were the main readers in the reading room where many prominent Malayalam dailies and weeklies were available. Though most of them had only primary education, they were a highly disciplined lot who read in perfect silence. Students and youth were the subscribers in the library. Detective novels in Malayalam and also translations from other languages had a great readership. Crime fiction was another genre which enjoyed a wide readership among young adults as murder mysteries always fired their imagination. Sherlock Holmes was an all-time hero of the young and the old alike. Dracula of Bram Stocker was in great demand. It was through this library that I read the memorable books of the master storytellers of Malayalam literature such as S K Pottekkatt, M T Vasudevan Nair, Vaikom Muhammed Basheer, Thakazhi, P Kesavadev, M Mukundan, and Perumbadavam Sreedharan, all writers who belonged to a particular pedigree in Malayalam literature. Interestingly, many old books did not have a beginning or end as a few pages from the beginning and end of the book would be missing. Despite such imperfections, we used to read such books with enthusiasm. We eagerly read those books without beginnings and ends. Some miscreants would scribble impolite remarks and nasty comments about the books on the margins while others would reveal the suspense through their unwanted comments which would kill our eagerness and enjoyment to read the book. Those old dust-filled books indeed have opened up a window to the world which was quite alien for a teenager. The stories fired the teenage reveries of a generation.

Sanmargodayam Library had a modest birth in the mid-fifties when K A Bahuleyan, my eldest brother-in-law and P K

Divakaran, my cousin; two young men of the village dreamed of a small library in the locality. For this, they collected old books which were taught in schools under non-detailed study. They eventually had a collection of close to one hundred books and a catalogue for the same was prepared. When they approached for a government grant, they were told that to qualify for the grant the library first of all should have a building and they should maintain a movement register of books. They found a small room alongside the Sankara Narayana Temple for the library from where it operated for many years till it was translocated to the present building owned by the library. In the early days, the Bahuleyan-Divakaran duo used to take the books in a cloth bag to the doorstep of the prospective readers for which they kept a register of subscribers. Later people were attracted to the library and began reading the books willingly. True to its name, which means 'the rise of the virtuous path', the Sanmargodayam Library has been a shining example of erudition, significantly contributing to the village's socio-cultural development and inspiring its people to embrace the power of knowledge.

During my high school days, our science teacher made arrangements for making available copies of *Eureka* and *Sastra Keralam*, two science publications published by Kerala Sastra Sahitya Parishad, an NGO engaged in popularizing science among students. Achan unhesitatingly agreed when I requested him to subscribe to *Sastra Keralam* and gave me enough money to subscribe. The journal opened up a new world of science in simple and fictional literature which was a great read.

Later, after completing my Pre-Degree, I took membership in the Ernakulam Public Library, following the advice of Premachandran, my well-wisher, friend and a librarian there. It was a huge book depository which surprised me with its size and the vast collection of English and Malayalam books on various subjects. It indeed has opened up an entirely different world of books. The distance from my home to the library was a deterrent which restricted my visits to the library to monthly once.

Navapuram, a hilly village in Kannur, North Kerala has recently been in the news, when a temple was dedicated to books with an image of a book in concrete as an idol, which is open to people irrespective of their caste and creed. Consecrated in October 2021, the temple is located in a sprawling 2-acre, picturesque landscape, which has a well-stocked library. Literary debates and film festivals are regularly held here. In the book, which is the idol, it is written, "God is knowledge, Broad thinking, humility, and wisdom are the way". This temple of books, which is conspicuous by the absence of priests and offerings, is perhaps the only one of its kind in the country which is the brainchild of Prapoyil Narayanan. The well-stocked library has over 5000 books. Quite interestingly, the four cornerstones of the temple were laid by Hindu, Christian, and Islamic clerics along with people's representatives and cultural activists. He has plans to set up art galleries, and creative space for writers to engage in discussions, reading sessions, and celebrations of books.

Kerala, the first fully literate state in India, is perhaps at the forefront of reading and nowhere else one can see a population so interested in reading newspapers and magazines that almost every household subscribes to at least one newspaper.

Recently UNESCO declared Kozhikode as India's first "City of Literature", a fitting recognition to a city with rich cultural, intellectual, and literary heritage. Kozhikode is the birth place or residence of many celebrated Malayalam literary figures. The numerous libraries, bookstores, and literary festivals are testaments to the city's literary legacy.

32. Malayalam: A Language in Transition

Every year February 21 is celebrated worldwide as International Mother Tongue Day, a day devoted to one's mother tongue, an occasion to reflect on its glory, a time to think about the state of the language in an era of the digital revolution in a globalized world and an opportunity to think loudly as how best one can preserve and protect our mother tongue.

By mother tongue what we mean is the first language we learn at home as a child, a language a person has spoken during his growing up years. This, otherwise described as native language, is the language in which our train of thought proceeds.

On this International Mother Tongue Day, I reflected on the plight of my mother tongue, Malayalam. It's a Dravidian language spoken by the people inhabiting the southernmost Indian state of Kerala and Lakshadweep, though people along the border states of Karnataka and Tamil Nadu also speak the language. Malayalam is believed to have originated from Sanskrit and Tamil and has been heavily borrowed from these two languages apart from Urdu, Arab, and some other languages. There is a considerable amount of difference between colloquial and formal language.

Malayalam is a living language that has evolved over centuries into one of the classic languages of India, a rare honor bestowed on the language in 2013. It's a language spoken by less than 35 million people as against 69 million people who speak Tamil. Malayalam has its dialect and grammar. However, today this beautiful regional language is encountering many challenges that appear to threaten its very survival.

Malayalam as a regional language has borrowed heavily from Sanskrit and the written language is spiced up with many Sanskrit words. Anyone who can speak and write Malayalam can take pride in the fact that the language has benevolently contributed many words to the English language which has become an integral part of the language. Words such as Ayurveda, coir, jackfruit, cashew, teak, curry, catamaran, and mango are just a few among them.

However, today Malayalam as a language is facing several challenges some of which have the potential to make it extinct. The craze of the urban middle class and the elite for English education has severely limited the growth of this language. In English medium schools, there's only one paper for Malayalam which in effect has adversely affected the use of the language both in spoken and written forms. The large-scale migration of the Malayalee population to other states and various foreign countries has curtailed the use of the language as a medium for communication. The Keralite diaspora in overseas countries is quite alien to the language. Grammar has been completely removed from the syllabus. During my school days, we had classes on Malayalam grammar from class 5 to 10 and we even had separate papers for grammar along with books for non-detailed study. A small, faded orange book on Malayalam grammar, *'Vyakarana Deepam'* by Prof. Mathew Ulakamthara, remains etched in my memory. This precious book was passed down to me by my elder sister, and its worn pages evoke a sense of nostalgia and gratitude. It was an excellent reference book on Malayalam grammar which I used till my 10th class. (Later when I joined for BSc at Sacred Heart College, Thevara, Kochi, I had the rare fortune of attending mesmerizing classes of Prof. Ulakamthara in Malayalam literature which attracted students even from Hindi classes). Quite interestingly many in the present generation do not even know that Malayalam has its numerals which fell into disuse many decades back. Now Malayalam digits are as good as dead and they can be seen only in ancient palm leaf manuscripts, horoscopes, and old books of Hindu hymns.

It may sound paradoxical to note that the first Malayalam grammar book *Malayalabhasha Vyakaranam* was written by a German missionary Herman Gundart in 1859.

Our over-dependence on English and scant regard for our mother tongue have drastically reduced the use of Malayalam in offices, educational institutions, and businesses. Even many parents belonging to the elite class considers their children speaking in Malayalam as below status and ask their children to speak in English. With the widespread use of social media platforms, a new genre called Manglish which is an awkward, strange, and nauseating mix of Malayalam and English words has come into existence. Today our urban youths and children use the language unhesitatingly. It's a shame that for the younger generations of Kerala, it's fashionable to say that they do not know Malayalam. As Thomas Gray has famously said, "Where ignorance is a bliss it is folly to be wise".

I am pained by the way we treat our mother tongue, a sort of stepmotherly treatment. Those who believe and consider Malayalam as an inferior lingo must realize that it's second to none. Many of the literary works of brilliance by wordsmith of Malayalam literature are today read and appreciated the world over in their translations either in English or other Indian or foreign languages. Raconteurs of Malayalam literature like Vaikom Muhammed Basheer, M T Vasudevan Nair, Thakazhi Sivasankara Pillai, O V Vijayan, S K Pottekkatt, Madhavikutty, M Mukundan, Anand, Uroob, and Kesavadev have an ardent fan following in other languages as their literary contributions are timeless. It's a matter of great pride for every Malayalee that the first Jnanpith Award, the highest literary honor in India, was won by the renowned Malayalam poet, G Sankara Kurup in 1965 for *Odakkuzhal*, his collection of poems. The literary genius of O V Vijayan and Basheer are comparable to the best in world literature and would have won the Nobel prize for literature had they written in English or other European languages. Writing in a lesser-known language spoken by a few in a tiny Indian state might have been a handicap in recognizing their literary genius.

It's now the responsibility of every Malayalee to encourage their children and grandchildren to learn and popularize Malayalam, a sweet and beautiful language lest it becomes extinct.

33. Willingdon Island: An Oasis of Quietude

Kochi is known worldwide by the descriptive appellation "Queen of the Arabian Sea" which is quite a fitting moniker for a breathtakingly beautiful landscape. Suppose Kochi is the "Queen of the Arabian Sea". In that case Willingdon Island is undoubtedly the "Crown of the Queen of Arabian Sea" which possesses the unique distinction as the largest man-made island in the country. With a host of amenities and connectivity by all means of transportation, this tiny island was a cynosure of all eyes.

A few months back I was passing through the famed Willingdon Island, the once bustling port city of Kerala. As I entered the port trust area the air turned gloomy all of a sudden and the whole landscape appeared dull and lifeless. Suddenly, a sense of alienation gripped me. But for a few cars, the Bristow Road, the main arterial road that connects the island with the mainland, wore a deserted look. The numerous roadside eateries that once crowded with people near the old Harbor Terminus station and port area were no longer visible. So were the noisy pack of laborers who worked in the Dock Labor Board (DLB). Most of the numerous warehouses near the wharf are in a state of neglect and disrepair. The area just in front of the station which used to be the taxi stand was almost vacant. The Harbor Terminus, till two decades ago abuzz with activities, was once the pride of Cochin. But now it is a dilapidated building in bad repair donning a haunted look with wild growth occupying the fringes of the platform. The station was renovated a few years back and with fanfare train services were launched on a limited scale between Ernakulam South and Harbor Terminus ferrying passengers in a diesel-powered train. Since the route was still not electrified many savored the idea of a travel though short in a diesel loco, enlivening nostalgic memories. This, however, was discontinued after a short while owing to poor passenger patronage because when the initial euphoria died down, people by and large abandoned the train and opted for travel by road. Till a few decades back the island was a luxurious landscape with the style and panache of a western country where she welcomed tourists with grace and aplomb.

However, in recent decades the island has been through so many vicissitudes including the shifting of the civil airport to Nedumbassery, the translocation of the seaport to Vallarpadom, and the gradual and almost complete cessation of passenger train services. All these have dealt a bodily blow to the once vibrant business capital of Kochi.

As I was driving through the vacant street my mind was flooded with good old memories of the island. I came to know about the history of Willingdon Island from my father, who had a photographic memory with vivid recollections. During his adolescent years more than a century back, when he was a student of St. Sebastian's School, Thoppumpady, opposite the school, in the middle of Kochi *kaayal*, there was a tiny, uninhabited landmass with the East Kochi on the other side. Occasionally, people used to go there in small wooden canoes to cut and collect grass which they would sell as fodder in the village market. It was only in the mid-thirties that the idea of a man-made island was conceptualized by expanding the existing tiny piece of land

In the midst of the Kochi backwaters, a man-made island was conceived by Sir Robert Bristow, a visionary British engineer, as a bold initiative to establish a modern seaport in Kochi. Sir Bristow was indeed a great visionary who could foresee far ahead of his times. But for this brilliant British engineer and his inventiveness and creativity, the fate of Kochi could have been different. He poignantly describes his fight against several odds and varied obstacles that he had to face, in his passionate memoir "Cochin Saga". (later to immortalize the name of this great visionary the arterial road of Willingdon Island was named Bristow Road after him). The island is an engineering marvel and was named after the Viceroy, Lord Willingdon, who commissioned its construction. Later in 1940, the island was connected to the mainland by the Venduruthy Bridge on the eastern side and Harbor Bridge on the western side. Achan shared in graphic details his experience of pedaling through the new bridges in youthful enthusiasm along with his few friends immediately after the inaugural event. Later a rail bridge was constructed alongside the Venduruthy Bridge connecting Harbor Terminus and Ernakulam South Station.

It was many years later that the Harbor Bridge was modified by providing a fascinating feature: a lift in the middle of the bridge which was operated with a pulley and iron rope system. This draw bridge mechanism was the first of its kind in Kerala and exemplifies the engineering mastery of the time. An important landmark, the Old Harbor Bridge has been nicknamed the "London Bridge of Kochi" owing to its British-era construction style. This enabled small ships to pass underneath the bridge to the adjacent Brunton Company on the other side of the bridge. The construction of the lift was an engineering challenge that left the people dumbfounded. The bridge along with the tall steel structures that form part of the hoist stands in good stead even now which has outlived its expected lifespan. Today the bridge along with the stupendous lift has become the icon of Kochi symbolizing a heritage we inherited from Sir Bristow.

My earliest memories of Willingdon Island are centered around Naval Base and INS Sanjivani where my mother would take me frequently for the treatment of several childhood diseases. I thoroughly enjoyed the bus ride from my native village Palluruthy to the Island which was hardly 5 KM away then. Those were the only rarest opportunities for me to go out and travel in buses. My journey became even more enjoyable as I traveled on buses that took the scenic route via Willingdon Island, circumnavigating the island and passing through key landmarks like the Terminus, port area, and Bristow Road, ultimately connecting at Vathuruthy, near the airport. In those days there was a KSRTC double-decker bus that plied between Willingdon Island and Palarivattom in which I aspired to travel but I could never. Back then the island was a vibrant business hub teeming with men engaged in innumerable activities. Then the island had an envious position as the only place in the world where a small manmade island was connected to the world beyond by road, rail, sea, and air transportation links- something unique to Willingdon Island. It was from the Harbor Terminus that I travelled for the first time in the crowded cattle class compartment of a train, along with Amma and our neighbors. It was a short journey to Thrissur for the onward journey by road to Guruvayoor in the late sixties. It was from the old Kochi airport on the island that I had my first flight in the mid-eighties and it was a trip to Goa to take up my first job. I can still picture the days when several Nissen huts lined one side of the railway line from Vathuruthy to the entry of Venduruthy bridge. These cylindrical steel structures were used as godowns by companies like Rallis India and FACT for storing fertilizers and chemicals. Till the turn of this century Willingdon Island had been a throbbing center of trade and commerce. Almost all-important shipping companies had their offices on the island.

The opulent and magnificent buildings like the Harbor Terminus railway station, the official bungalow of Sir Bristow, the Headquarters of Cochin Port Trust, the Customs House, the Port Hospital, and the old Malabar Hotel, all these buildings are architectural marvels which combine the best of modern and medieval architecture. Unlike other parts of Kochi, the Island has wide and neatly built road which crisscrossed the city, wide and beautifully designed footpaths, the pavements lined by huge Gulmohar trees; the island in short was an idyllic landscape with a stunning view of the sprawling city and the marvelous sight of the west Kochi. Once an all-pervasive quaint charm lingered in the atmosphere. The landscape was enchantingly alluring. The island offers a picturesque view of boats on Vembanad Lake, surrounded by lush greenery and charming bridges, but the breathtaking view of the sunset is the highlight. But no more. Now it's a neglected area with abandoned godowns and unused buildings which imparts the appearance of a ghost town to the island. This beautiful island, however, offers tremendous potential to be developed as a tourist destination.

34. The Fascinating Story of Watches in India

Watches in India have a fascinating history which began with the British Empire. Through decades watches have undergone a great amount of transformation. Recent years have witnessed the birth of smartwatches capable of performing tasks of unbelievable nature. In keeping with the growing requirements of elite class, leading watch manufacturers came up with smartwatches which apart from displaying time and date, are capable of multiple functions like internet telephony and almost all functions of a smartphone. There is an ever-growing popularity for smartwatches the world over which has revolutionized the way we use watches.

The history of watches in India dates back to the 1900's. The erstwhile Maharaja of Patiala had a penchant for luxury watches and he had a huge collection of luxury watches. Those were hand-crafted watches in gold with the enameled image of the Maharaja engraved on one side. Those watches became part of best-loved regalia.

In those days watches were used mainly by the most affluent for whom it was yet another icon of the aristocracy. Back then almost all watches were Swiss-made. Designer watches were quite common among Indian Royalty, which performed difficult and multiple functions like built-in alarms, and a moon phase as a chronograph with a minute repeater. Indian Maharajas of those days had a strong passion for pocket watches of Vacheron Constantin, a Swiss luxury watch manufacturer founded in 1755 that provided the highest quality luxury watches.

In late forties, Achan bought a Sowar Prima brand mechanical watch manufactured by West End Watch Company of Swiss which was launched in 1917. It had a small round dial with a Stainless-Steel strap, a leading brand in those days. He used it for many years until he bought another one for my elder brother in the early sixties. It was ENICAR, another well-known brand that was slightly larger than Sowar Prima. My brother told Achan that ENICAR with its large dial looked awkward on his slender wrist and requested Achan to exchange the new watch with the decade-old Sowar Prima which Achan agreed. Even after more than 75 years, the watch is in immaculate condition and working perfectly with astonishing accuracy withstanding the vagaries of time and so is its younger cousin ENICAR. My brother is still keeping this rare piece as a prized possession though many people approached him offering handsome prices for this vintage watch.

1961 was a watershed year in the history of Indian watches as it was this year Hindustan Machine Tools better known by its acronym HMT started its first state-of-the art watch manufacturing facility in Bangalore in collaboration with Citizen Watch, Japan. This has revolutionized the Indian watch market like never before as watches hitherto affordable only to the riches became a common household item and became ubiquitous. HMT watches soon conquered the Indian market, propelled by huge demand and the dominance of Swiss watches was challenged. With the tagline "TIMEKEEPERS OF THE NATION" HMT watches soon became a dream product of urban elite and rural youth.

HMT was the brainchild of our first Prime Minister Jawaharlal Nehru, for which technical cooperation was provided by Citizen Watch. HMT factory was completed in 1963 and inaugurated on 15th August 1963, truly reflecting the spirit of a nation. HMT was heralding a new era when it produced 500 HMT *Citizen* for men and 300 number HMT *Sugata* for ladies. The first batch was launched by Nehru himself. *Kohinoor, Neeraj, Pilot*, and *Jhelum* were much sought-after variants. HMT *Janata* was indeed a people's watch in all its meaning, both affordable and durable. Former Prime Minister, Mrs. Indira Gandhi was a great admirer of HMT *Janata* watches. HMT *Pilot* was made exclusively for Fighter Pilots of the Indian Air Force who participated in the 1971 Indo-Pak war while HMT *Jawan* was for noncommissioned officers of the Indian Army. In those days many companies gifted HMT watches with customized company logos as mementos to commemorate milestone achievements. In 1984 to celebrate the occasion of Asian games in Delhi, HMT launched a special edition HMT *Appu* with the Asiad mascot Appu, the elephant on the dial which was a rare collector's item. In the sixties and the seventies HMT watches adorned the wrists of the Indian public. As a teenager, I strongly aspired for an HMT watch, the one with a sparkling white dial with a black strap which Babu master, our physics teacher had. A few of my friends in high school had HMT watches. My father promised me a watch if I scored good marks in my Pre Degree. Though I could not fare better he gifted me a watch as he promised, it was not an HMT but a large golden Hegde & Golay (H&G) watch with a blue dial which looked awkward on my slender hand.

At the time, international brands like West End, and Anglo-Swiss were ruling the market, HMT proved itself as an instant hit. However, the wealthy continued to use expensive watches like Rado, Rolex, Seiko, and Citizen. The emergence of Quartz and electronic watches dealt a heavy blow to the plans of HMT.

Slowly by the early seventies, the old hand-wound watches gave way to automatic watches. With a sense of surprise, people accepted automatic watches, as they need not wind the watch every morning which for many had become part of everyday life. By the early eighties, the watch industry had been for yet another surprise product, the battery-driven watches which were powered by minute button cells.

By the mid-eighties, Tata Group ventured into the watch industry which by then had been monopolized by HMT. Many were skeptical about the entry of Tatas into the watch market which many considered as a misadventure because it was quite difficult to penetrate a market dominated by HMT. But in a short time "Titan" became a household brand in India slowly but steadily relegating its arch-rival HMT to second. Today Titan smartwatches are available with features and quality similar to Apple and Samsung.

The switch over to Quartz watches by competitors, while HMT still focused on mechanical watches, was one of the many reasons for its downfall. Mounting losses to the tune of 2500 crore rupees finally forced the government to shut down the once popular watch company in 2016 which marked the unceremonious exit of the "Timekeepers of the Nation" which once fascinated millions of consumers both in India and abroad.

35. Unni *Aasaan:* The Guiding Light on My Path of Knowledge

It was sometime in mid-1965 that I was initiated into the sacred world of letters when I was hardly four. On a fine morning which was a *Vidyarambham* day, Amma took me to the nearby Sri Venkatachalapathy Temple, and the priest in an atmosphere filled with *bhakti*, wrote Ha, Ri, Sree the first three Malayalam letters on the tip of my outstretched tongue using a golden needle. The ritual was performed with all the sanctity attached to the ceremony. This was to be followed by writing the Malayalam alphabet in raw rice which was spread on a brass tray and the priest guided my hands holding my tender fingers tightly with his thick and fleshy fingers. Many children who were made to go through the same rituals were crying inconsolably though I kept quiet throughout.

After a short while, Amma took me to the nearby *"Aasaan Kalari"*, a forerunner of the present-day nursery school, run by Unni *Aasaan*. When we reached there *Aasaan*, the Master, was sitting on the floor of the tiny veranda of his small thatched house. A few more children of my age were gathered there accompanied by their parents or grandparents. I looked around with a mixed feeling of awe and wonder. As instructed by

Amma, I touched his feet with both hands as a mark of respect and then gave the *dakshina*, a 25 Paisa coin along with an arecanut wrapped inside betel leaves. I held the *dakshina* tightly in my hands with my palms folded in supplication. He received it with a smile and gently touched my head as a gesture of blessing. Thereafter *Aasaan* made me repeat the act of writing letters in raw rice spread over the floor. I looked around with a vacant expression and little did I know that I was indeed beginning a lifelong journey through the world of letters, a journey which I continue to pursue even this day with enthusiasm.

From that day onwards, I was taught by *Aasaan* for the coming one and a half years, till I was admitted to class 1. Those were among the blissful days in my life. There were almost a dozen students and every morning all of us would assemble in the front courtyard of *Aasaan*, which was behind the famous Sree Bhavaneeswara Temple. From there we would walk to the *Kudippallikkoodam* which was located a little away. *Aasaan* was very particular about his costumes and he always dressed in a white spotless *mundu* and white shirt with a *naadan* (shawl) on his shoulders. A long crook handle umbrella (*kaalan kuda*) with a wooden handle was an inseparable part of himself which was a necessity in the hot summers and rainy monsoon. While walking, his black leather footwear constantly produced "tup" "tup" sound which I greatly enjoyed. I too tried to imitate the sound with my Bata rubber slippers. *Aasaan* used *metiyadi*, a pair of traditional-style wooden chappals made of inexpensive lightweight wood which he used while walking in his courtyard.

The *Kalari* was located around a mile south of where *Aasaan* lived and we walked the distance while talking endlessly. On either side of the village path, there were a few small houses and any landmarks worth mentioning were completely absent. On the way, there was a tiny tea shop where the village elders would gather. While sipping hot tea they shared news and gossip. Many of them smoked beedi the smell of which left me sneezing. They wore printed *mundus* which would be folded above the knee and bare-chested. On seeing *Aasaan*, they would unfold their *mundu* which was an expression of respect. A peaceful silence lingered in the atmosphere which would occasionally be broken by the chirping of birds and the sound of thrashing wet clothes on washing stones by village women. Grey smoke could be seen billowing from the kitchens of small houses that lined the path. At home, the elderly women wore *mundu* and blouse which exposed a major part of the belly. In many places, the village alley sneaked through the courtyard of others. Boundaries were separated by fences made of thatched coconut fronds but most homesteads were devoid of gates. On the way lived Kumaran, whom I considered a fearsome person as he always kept a machete and he made a living by plucking coconuts. He stammered while he spoke which earned him the moniker *nja, nja, nja* Kumaran. My friend told me many imaginary stories about his unruly acts which scared me though those were far from the truth.

The *kalari* was housed inside a small chapel called Chackalath *Kurisupura*, roomy enough to accommodate 15-20 kids. The nondescript building had a tiled roof with a small wooden cross atop and large windows through which fresh cool wind gushed in during hot summer days. The floor was plastered with a thick layer of cow dung paste beneath which was the floor made of red laterite powder. In many places, the floor would be bulged through which white mushrooms propped up. Along the corners and the joints where the walls met the floor, mounds of termites would be a regular occurrence. At the farther end of the chapel, in a small room separated by grilled doors, the idol of the patron saint St. Francis of Assisi and Mother Mary were kept inside glass cages. I firmly believe that I received in abundance the blessings of the Saints which later in my life kindled the passion in me for reading and writing. A few decades ago, the old chapel was demolished, and a new one was built in its place. For the past few years, I made it a practice in my family to take my children and the children of my nephews and nieces to the chapel before the commencement of their examinations to seek the blessings of the Saints and to light candles. The pipeline near the chapel demarcated two villages namely Rameswaram and Palluruthy. Later a road was constructed which was appropriately named Pipe Line Road. Near the chapel, a part of the pipeline remained exposed as it passed over a large dried-up pond.

My two elder sisters would always dress me up in the best clothes and also made me wear a light blue fedora. They often applied eyeliner in my eyes which very often attracted sarcastic comments from my classmates. Most of them were hailing from very poor backgrounds and for them mocking me was a favorite pastime, though we were full of cheerful bonhomie.

Aasaan personified the best of teachers as he taught us each Malayalam letter one by one with utmost patience and love. He would begin his teaching with *"Akshara Mala"*, the string of letters in order written on a dried palm leaf. It was indeed a marvelous sight to see as he wrote each letter legibly on the palm leaf with an iron stylus, (*naaraayam*) made of iron. First, the broad end of the palm leaf would be folded elegantly which would resemble the knot of a necktie with its narrow end neatly trimmed. He would hold the stylus firmly vertically downwards with all his fingers and then he would write each letter on the leaf. Thereafter the leaf would be subjected to a unique treatment to make the letters visible. For this, he would mix wood charcoal with water cabbage (*kula payal*) which had succulent leaves full of water. The palm leaf would be smeared evenly with this paste, then it would be wiped off completely after a while using a cloth. As we looked in surprise, thick, black letters would emerge on the palm leaf which would be our textbook for the coming few weeks. When we fully understand the inscriptions on the leaf, another one would be added with the remaining part of the *akshara maala*. In due course, we would have a bundle of such palm leaf with full of inscriptions which

Aasaan would carefully tie together with a twine. Inside the *kalari* Asaan made us sit on the floor in a long single row facing the window on the north. *Aasaan* used to walk back and forth in the room wielding a *chooral* which he seldom used. Through the wide-open windows, we had an unhindered view of the dried-up pond and the exposed pipeline that passed above, and beyond the *vellaripadam* where cucumbers grew.

Aasaan had no fixed fee for his service which was more of a selfless effort. Every Saturday we would give him 4 Ana as *dakshina* equivalent to 25 paise by the present reckoning which would be the sole income for his family. A few amongst us were so poor that they couldn't afford even this modest amount, as they were leading a life of penury and starvation. He never insisted on *dakshina* from his students, and we voluntarily paid the amount. Some pupils would gift him small articles like vegetables collected from their kitchen garden which he received with gratitude. He was greeted with great respect and love by the villagers, an honor he rightly deserved for his selfless services to three generations of the village. He passed away on a sunny morning in the early 1980s as an unsung hero who initiated the people of the sleepy village into the limitless world of knowledge. He was a dedicated apostle of pedagogy. He enlightened me on accepting learning as a lifelong process which later in my life served as a guiding light. *Aasaan*, as my first Guru, played a foundational role in shaping my educational journey. My salutations to the great Guru who opened to me the doors to the vast world of knowledge.

36. *Pappadam*: The Quintessential Culinary Accompaniment

In Kerala, one can never imagine a hearty meal without the crumbly, crunchy, golden yellow *Pappadam*. Despite its fragility and brittleness, it is a quintessential accompaniment that goes well with both vegetarian and non-vegetarian dishes. Though occasions may vary, *Pappadam* is an important and indispensable part of traditional cuisine. With its distinct shape, size, appearance, and flavor, *Pappadam* has an individuality of its own and stands out from rest of the innumerable items served.

They are invariably circular though the sizes may vary from the normal palm-sized one, to the small coin-sized Guruvayoor *Pappadam*, to the rarely used mammoth-sized *"aana Pappadam"*. Variants of tongue tingling *Pappadam* are available like the spicy garlic *Pappadam* and peppery *Mulaku Pappadam*.

Though *Pappadam* has always been an excellent part of many kinds of meals, probably the best combination is with *Payasam*, especially *Parippu Payasam*. Finely crushed *Pappadam* mixed with *Njali poovan* banana and hot *Payasam* served on a plantain leaf is the high point of a traditional *sadya*; a mouthwatering gastronomic delight, an awesome mash-up. Quite funnily, the *Pappadam, Pazham, Payasam,* combo as a rule, is served toward the fag end of the lavish meal. The crunching sound and the aroma that fill the air as we collectively break *Pappadam* into pieces at a *sadya,* preceding the delightful consumption of *Payasam,* is truly amazing. Rice *Puttu* mixed with finely crushed *Pappadam* is an equally wonderful combination, where the slightly salty *Pappadam* imparts a unique taste and incredible flavor to the rice *Puttu.* During my childhood years, there used to be a small village tea shop in our neighborhood, which was housed in the front veranda of a small thatched house furnished with an old wooden bench and a desk. The shop, staffed by a woman we affectionately called '*chayapeedikakkari*', was a local institution renowned for its delectable *Puttu* and *Pappadam* combination, paired with *Kattan Chaya,* a beloved brew cherished not only by the locals but also by people from neighboring areas. A splendid experience indeed. The shop was located by the side of the jetty in the lake and customers were mostly fishermen and women who inhabited the other side of the lake but daily ferried to the mainland for selling fish in the local market.

Pappadam making in Kerala is the traditional avocation (*kula thozhil*) of a particular community, the tribe called "*Pappada pandarangal*'/ "*Pappada Chetty*" who have migrated to Kerala from Tamil Nadu and nuances of the making of this much sought after culinary item being a well-kept secret handed down generations.

During my younger days, a *Pappada Chetty* whom we respectfully addressed as "*Pappadakkaran Muthalaly*" used to visit our home once or twice every week with his top-quality home-made *Pappadam.* Back then a pack of ten cost 10 paise. Occasionally, during festive seasons like Onam, he would bring *Mulaku Pappadam* which had a pungent flavor of chili which we savored heartily.

Traditionally the *Pappadam* is prepared by flash frying in boiling coconut oil, which imparts the characteristic golden yellow color with innumerable bubbles of varying sizes. During my childhood days, after frying the *Pappadam*, Amma used to pour a spoonful of the dark colored leftover oil over the rice which imparted a delicious taste and aroma to the food. "*Pappada Vada*" is a conventional finger food made of *Pappadam*. This is prepared by dipping *Pappadam* in a dough of rice flour containing various spices like chili powder, turmeric powder, asafetida, and a generous amount of sesame seeds and then flash-fried in oil. Hot and crunchy *Pappada vada* with hot tea would be a wonderful miscellany. *Pappadam* can also be roasted either on a hot pan or by exposing it directly to medium flame which would have numerous charred black spots on it. Since oil is not used, roasted ones are relished by the health-conscious. *Chutta Pappadam* along with *podiyari kanji*, the rice gruel made from broken rice, would be part of the strict dietary regimen suggested by the village doctor whenever we would be down with fever in our growing up years. Those were the only times when I hated *Pappadam*. *Pappadam* cut into small pieces and then fried with chopped onions and chili powder is yet another variant of *Pappadam* which along with *kanji* constitute a gorgeous dish.

Pappadam is made of dough of urad dal (black gram) flour along with rice and tapioca flour leavened with sesame oil, salt, and a pinch of *pappadakkaram*, the baking soda. In the traditional method, the prepared dough is kneaded, rolled out, and then cut into small pieces. These pieces are then flattened into thin, moon-like circles using a long, narrow rolling pin on a rolling board, creating the distinctive shape of *Pappadam*. While this traditional technique is still used, modern machines have also been introduced to streamline the process. *Pappadam* is then dusted with black gram flour to prevent them from sticking to each other and then sun-dried. Now the *Pappadam* is ready for use. For Keralites, *Pappadam* is more than just a food item - it's a cultural icon that embodies the rich heritage and distinctive culinary traditions of the region. It's a symbol of pride and identity, deeply woven into the fabric of Kerala's gastronomic legacy.

37. Classes Underneath the Banyan Trees

Banyan trees are somehow inexplicably and inseparably connected with the temples of Kerala. If you spot a banyan tree somewhere on your way, you can conclude for sure that a temple is not far off. The ubiquitous *Arayaal* protected with a brick or granite base filled with sand, the *aalthara*, is a constant presence in front of almost all temples in Kerala, irrespective of the presiding deity. In Hindu mythology, the Banyan tree is treated among *Deva Vriksha*, the divine trees, and many qualities which no other tree can claim, are believed to have been possessed by them. One such popular belief is that it produces more oxygen in comparison to other trees of similar size and build, which has been later corroborated by scientific studies. From very ancient times it was believed that taking a few '*pradakshina*' around banyan trees would freshen up the mind and energize the body of the devotees and in many temples circumambulating the banyan tree is part of the ritual. In ancient temples, like the Sree Kurumba Temple in Kodungalloor, Thrissur, there is an abundance of centuries old, mammoth-sized banyan trees, all around the temple in its sprawling compound. Some of them would surprise the onlookers with their sheer size and by the strong and massive prop roots that hang down, some of which touching the ground beneath.

S D P Y B H S, the school where I had my secondary education, shared its playground with the vast temple grounds of Sree Bhavaneeswara Temple to which the school belonged. Right in front of the temple on either side of the enormous courtyard, there stand two huge banyan trees that spread their strong branches all around creating a dense canopy. The small heart-shaped leaves of the banyan trees danced incessantly and uncontrollably even in a gentle breeze. While moving, the leaves produced a peculiar kind of crackling sound which could be heard from a distance.

During sweltering summer days, our teachers would guide us to the shadows of the trees and the mighty among us would hastily arrange the wooden blackboard, its tripod stand, and the wooden chair of the teacher. We would sit around the teacher in two or three semicircular rows. The classes under the trees would be usually in the afternoon. As the evening sun casts its shaft of light over us, we would move ourselves into the shades.

It was indeed a jasmine-scented memory of us sitting in the cool and dark canopy of the banyan trees and repeating the poem in perfect unison that the teacher recited. We vied with one another to recite the poem in the loudest possible sound. Since no other classes were there in the immediate vicinity teacher gave us the liberty to speak loudly in the class. Listening to the teacher while enjoying the cool wind in those hot summer afternoons was a delightful experience to be enjoyed. And in those classrooms without walls, we enjoyed real freedom.

Classes under the banyan trees were refreshing and enjoyable experience for both the students and teachers. Under each banyan tree, two or even three classes would be arranged. Language classes and skill development classes like crafts would be normally arranged. While we would be engaged in the making of coir mattresses and small toys using strips cut out of cigarette packets, teachers would use the opportunity to exchange gossip. The gentle breeze saturated with oxygen would provide a salubrious environment that stimulated our mind and body. Occasionally, the crows nesting in the treetops would soil our books and clothing with their droppings.

Then we had many preposterous beliefs which had been passed down from our seniors. One such belief was that if one could catch a falling green leaf of the banyan tree before it touched the ground, our wishes would be fulfilled. Naively believing such absurd stories, we would hurl stones at the tree and would waste our time during the interval, as a solution to escape the thrashing by the math teacher for not doing homework. From the staff room, he would have watched our adventurous feats. Back in the classroom, he would punish us on two separate counts, one for not completing homework and another for throwing stones at the banyan tree and wasting time and an extra beating for impropriety.

Age has left its impression on both the banyan trees as they became weaker. A substantial portion of the branches of both the trees have been cut down recently to construct a *nadapandal* in front of the temple. The onslaught has further weakened the already frail trees.

According to Hindu belief, four types of trees are considered sacred; 1. *Athy* (fig); 2. *Ithy* (*Ficus gibbosa*); 3. *Peraal* (banyan trees) and 4. *Arayaal* (peepal tree). It was under the peepal tree that Buddha attained enlightenment and hence the tree came to be known as Bodhi tree.

Unlike other trees, banyan trees are capable of producing oxygen during night hours also by absorbing carbon dioxide, in the complete absence of sunlight, through a unique phenomenon called Crassulacean Acid Metabolism (CAM). Unsurprisingly these trees occupy a central position in many Indian villages and often the Gram Sabha are held under the comforts of banyan trees.

Unlike other trees, the rustling noise of the peepal leaves is unique and is accompanied by a mild cracking sound. It is said that the peculiar crackling sound is due to the bursting of calcium crystals called cystoliths which are embedded within the heart-shaped peepal leaves. The indolent amongst us would doze off, listening to the rumblings of the leaves and caressed by the gentle afternoon breeze. Come rainy days and our freedom to huddle under the shades of the banyan tree would be snatched away from us for the following six months. When it rained the trees produced a different kind of sound which mingled with the noise of the downpour, creating a unique musical pitter-patter. Occasionally a few parrots visited the trees to feed on the seed-encased berries. We would be overjoyed at the thought of sitting beneath the banyan trees on a fine day enjoying the verdure in harmony with nature.

Most banyan and peepal trees in temples and sacred groves would be protected by a brick wall (*aalthara*) and the two trees in the courtyard of our school are no exception.

38. Kerosene Lamps and Petromax in an Age of Darkness

In our sleepy village by the sea in old Kochi, electricity was a rare luxury and became available only by the mid-sixties. Till then only the stretch along the National Highway had been electrified and had street lights, with a few houses along the roadside provided with electricity. Till electricity connections reached, we spent our nights in the dim lights of kerosene lamps. Those lamps were available in numerous sizes and shapes. We had half a dozen such lamps made of brass, while the poor had aluminum lamps and the poorest had empty glass bottles modified as lamps with a cotton wick that would be inserted inside through a small hole made on top of the lid. Apart from the brass lamps, we had a large chimney lamp made of glass and a hurricane lamp as our prized possessions. The massive all-glass chimney lamp was a very old one used in Achan's *tharavad* and while sharing the family properties *Ilayachan*, my father's younger brother gifted it to me. A chimney lamp normally has a metal body at the bottom called fount which is the reservoir that holds the kerosene and the wick above would be encased in a glass enclosure. There's a mechanism to adjust the light intensity by turning the wick raiser knob which allows the wick to go up or down. While the chimney lamp illuminated the long veranda, the brass lamps lit other rooms like the drawing room, kitchen, and dining area. During the twilight hours, the *Nilavilakku* with 5 long wicks filled with oil would spread its golden glow in the spacious drawing room. My elder sister and I would huddle around the chimney and we would do our homework under its flickering light. It was under its dim light that we used to play carroms. On many occasions, the unexpectedly arrived wind would put out the kerosene lamps. Amma would always keep a matchbox handy at her arm's length. Every evening my sister was tasked with the dirty job of cleaning all the kerosene lamps of soot, using clothes and refilling them with kerosene which she did assiduously.

It was during the night before the wedding of a young woman in our neighborhood that I happened to see a petromax for the first time. For us, the children, the petromax was indeed a wonder lamp that aroused our curiosity. Later such petromax became very common in functions like temple festivals, marriage, and rituals associated with death in the village. What fired our inquisitiveness was the white, soft, oblong-shaped mesh called the mantle. Fixing the mantle in place and lighting the petromax were prodigious pieces of work that skilled elders did with utmost patience and care. The light in a petromax is produced by the burning mantle. The day before the marriage of my eldest sister, three petromax lamps were brought in, one in the *kalavara*, the makeshift kitchen where various items for the *sadya* were being readied, one hung in the middle of the huge Pandal, and the third one was kept as standby. While one neighbor was readying the petromax lamps, out of childlike curiosity, I gently touched the mantle which was so soft that it suddenly disintegrated without leaving a trace. My unwanted behavior had invited the wrath of the relatives and I heard someone screaming that to buy a new mantle one has to pedal 3 miles to Thoppumpady, the nearby small town.

I always viewed petromax in wonderment and considered it as a magic lamp descended from another world. In the early sixties, our village had a couple of shops that provided petromax for rent along with various supplies required for the making of a Pandal and wooden chairs. During festival days in the nearby temples, these lamps were in high demand to light up the large number of temporary stalls selling items from tea to toys, which would be erected along the fringes of the vast temple grounds. The large shops would be lit up with petromax whilst the smaller ones, the smoke-spewing, oil-smelling kerosene lamps.

"Petromax", is the brand name of a special type of pressurized kerosene lamp which derived its name by combining "petroleum "and "Max Graetz", the inventor of the lamp. It has a metal body with a large circular fuel tank and a glass cage that covers the mantle from which the bright white light emanates. In past decades, many accidents have been reported involving the bursting of petromax.

Half a century back, such kerosene lamps lighted up our nights and enlivened our lives. The smoldering lamps with flickering flame had an esoteric appeal. By the mid-seventies, by then electricity became ubiquitous, petromax, hurricane lamps, and kerosene lamps eclipsed into nostalgic memories.

39. *Vazhivilakkukal*: The Village Street Lights Through Decades

During my growing up years in the late sixties and early seventies, to reach my home, which was located in the interior part of the village, one had to walk close to a mile through the winding alleys. Palluruthy Veli was the bus stop nearest to my home and to reach there we would walk through the meandering village paths lined with trees, fences, and thick undergrowth where snakes and rats inhabited during the night. Deviating from the alleyways, we often took shortcuts which invariably passed through the compounds of many homesteads. It was a time when the village was a huge conglomeration of borderless homesteads. Some people demarcated their property with fences but none had gates barring a few rich villagers. We walked freely and merrily through the neighbor's land, an act that no one questioned. Similarly, many people in the neighborhood passed through our compound to avoid the long distance to the nearby church and market. We enjoyed unbridled freedom of movement. But by nightfall, the landscape would change as the entire locality would be enveloped by a thick blanket of darkness. As a rule, the villagers avoided travelling through these paths after nightfall as they feared unexpected attacks from snakes and street dogs who would reign over the area. We moved after sunsets only if it was unavoidable and, in such circumstances, people would illuminate their paths ahead with a lighted *choottu*; dried coconut leaves bundled together which they would sway back and forth to keep it aglow. We had a battery-powered "Eveready" torch at home which Achan had brought from Delhi during one of his annual leaves, which was a rarity back then.

Utsavam, (the annual temple festival) in the nearby Sree Bhavaneeswara Temple was one such rare occasion during which we would travel to the temple ground at night in small groups of neighbors comprising men, women, and children. One among the menfolk would lead us from the front by walking ahead of the others carrying a lighted *choottu*, lighting the path for his followers to follow. As we would near the temple, the coconut torch would be extinguished and it would be hidden safely among the bushes to be recovered later during our return journey.

Along the main thoroughfares, there were a few electric street lamps that hung down from wooden posts on a curved metal holder. The 40 W incandescent bulbs would be fitted in the center of a white circular shade which would spread light only in its immediate vicinity.

One summer afternoon, my playmate Robert said that the Panchayat was installing a new street lamp, the *vazhivilakku* as it is called in Malayalam, in our locality which came as a pleasant surprise for us. We excitedly ran towards the spot where the new street lamp was being installed. It was installed on the spot where the narrow path leading from my house merged with a wide but shallow pond, which we had to cross, to continue our forward journey to school, market, and bus stop. The street lamp comprised of a metal cage covered with glass panels on all four sides with one openable which served as the door through which the lighted kerosene lamp would be placed inside. The cage terminated at the top in a small, pointed chimney, featuring openings on all sides to allow smoke to escape. The entire cage was fixed atop a 6-7-foot-long wooden pole. We eagerly waited for the sunset. Just before sunset, a short medium-built, bare-chested man wearing a shabby *mundu* came, carrying a small wooden ladder, a cloth bag containing a bottle of kerosene, a few pieces of wicks and an old piece of cloth blackened with soot. He carefully leaned his ladder against the lamppost, slowly climbed up, opened the glass door, filled the lamp with kerosene, a new wick inserted through the nozzle, and lighted the lamp with a matchstick. The burning lamp was carefully placed inside the cage and he climbed down after closing the door. By now a small crowd of children, neighborhood women, and a few elders had gathered around the lamppost. We cheered the man with an uproarious outburst and remained there until nightfall, when as darkness descended on the scene, the lamp glowed with a golden flame which lit up the area around the lamp. Thereafter, it became a familiar sight for the villagers to see the man coming every evening and lighting the lamp, whether rain or shine. On some days, the lamp would continue to flicker till daybreak. Back then kerosene appeared as a crystal-clear liquid like water. It was only later that the blue color was added to the colorless paraffin oil as a safeguard against its possible misuse as an adulterant in diesel.

Similar glass-covered street lamps were also installed in a few other locations, one at Chirackal junction was an antique piece with an old-fashioned, cast-iron post with decorative designs on top and all along its length.

Our part of the village had been electrified only by the late sixties. It has revolutionized our life in unimaginable ways. Apart from ours, only very few houses were initially electrified. Our home was equipped with a pair of Orient brand ceiling fans, which Achan had brought back from Delhi, and a tube light, a luxury item in those days. On most days the single tube light which was fixed in the drawing room would not work due to voltage fluctuations. It would flicker uncontrollably, then someone, mostly my elder sister or brother, would turn the starter a few times and then it would light for some time. We would wait till late in the night for the tube light to come on spreading silvery white light and fans to work properly. Back then electricity in Kochi was supplied by Cochin Electric Company P Ltd (CECPL), a private entity owned and operated by S Kodar, a Jewish businessman and philanthropist who has made lasting contributions to the socio-cultural milieu of Kochi. The company which started on July 1, 1926, provided excellent services, at a time when technology was outdated. Later in the late 1970s, Kerala State Electricity Board took over Cochin Electric Company which had its office at Thoppumpady.

Other electric gadgets like mixers, fridges, TVs, and washing machines became a part of our everyday life much later. In the early eighties, as part of urbanization efforts, the Cochin Corporation transitioned from incandescent bulbs to sodium vapor lamps, and more recently, to LED lamps along all main roads and by lanes.

40. Kishore & Rahim: Echoes of Lost Innocence

Had he lived, Kishore would have turned 63 in August 2024. He was the youngest of the three children of the Dasan-Padmakshy couple, who stayed in a tiny thatched house with two matchbox-sized rooms next to our homestead. Our families maintained good neighborly relationships and Amma used to extend all possible help to them. The entire family relied on the modest weekly amount Dasan Chetan provided, more as a gesture of goodwill than a fulfillment of his familial responsibilities as a husband and father. This was because he had a second family, a wife and three children, elsewhere, where he spent the prime of his life. His relationship with Padmakshy Chechi was strained, a result of his divided loyalties and priorities. They lived under perpetual poverty and a square meal meant a distant dream for them and very often Amma helped her with cash and food. Occasions were not rare when her children used to sleep in our house during rainy days when their own house would be leaking profusely.

Kishore was almost my age and he was a handsome, fair-skinned, and highly energetic boy. During the day time, we played together often in my house or sometimes underneath the shade of the huge neem tree that stood in the courtyard of the nearby Puthanpurackal family. Usually, kids from the vicinity also joined us during our playtime. However, I had an abiding friendship with Kishore and we were an inseparable duo, as if we had two bodies but one soul. His elder brother Joshy also joined us in our playing sessions. We would be merrily engaged in various village games and enjoying it thoroughly. The plays varied from *goli*, seven stones, and hide and seek while grown-up boys played football, *kuttiyum kolum* (boy and cane), and hopscotch. Hide and seek was the favorite game of the smaller kids and we made use of every inch of our house and every space which provided enough room for us to hide. Many such hiding spots proved to be dangerous and stories of children being asphyxiated to death when hidden in the most unlikely and dangerous areas, like inside wooden rice boxes and almirah, were doing their rounds.

It was a bright and sunny summer afternoon. The sky was clear and the atmosphere was hot but pleasant. The time was around 3 pm. As usual, Kishore came to my house after lunch and I invited him to play hide and seek which he accepted with alacrity. Since Amma knew well that he had hardly eaten anything for lunch, she offered him *appam*, which she had prepared for breakfast. As he accepted it, his eyes brightened up with pleasure, and he started nibbling it. As I was so impatient that I could not wait for him to finish the *appam*, with half-eaten *appam* in his hands we started the game. First, it was Kishore's turn to hide while I would seek him after counting up to ten. I counted ten with my face turned towards a coconut tree and eyes tightly closed. This gave him ample time to find a suitable place to hide. As I finished counting, I opened my eyes and started searching for him. I searched him in the usual hiding places, like in the bushes, behind the trunk of the huge mango tree in the front courtyard, in the *kulippura*, the temporary thatched bathroom of those days, which had no roof over it, and practically in every nook and corner of the house. Despite my best efforts, I couldn't find his hiding spot. Time was running out. I searched in vain for him for about ten-fifteen minutes. This was quite unusual and unexpected because we knew each other's hiding places very well, from where we would emerge in a whiff of a second, springing surprise to the seeker. As time was moving fast, I became a bit nervous and told Amma, who was taking her routine afternoon nap, that Kishore had gone missing. Amma rushed out, wasting no time, and raised the alarm. My two elder sisters joined her, all of them yelling at the top of their voices. "Kishore, Kishore… where are you? Please come out of your hiding spot." But there was no response. The high-decibel bawling brought people from the vicinity and in no time a crowd formed in front of my house. By now nervousness gripped everyone. Padmakshy Chechi, who came there hearing the vociferous commotion, started wailing. Amma tried to console her by hiding her own anxiety and nervousness. Someone in the crowd suggested searching the pond, which was located in the *kannimoola* of our compound. The deep and large pond had no fencing around it. On many occasions, we used to play games on the bank of the pond. On that fateful day, Kishore selected the root-covered bottom part of the coconut palm, which stood on the edge of the pond, to hide. While he hid there waiting for me to finish the counting, he slid himself down and fell into the pond. By now the crowd swelled up. Women started crying. It was Padmanabhan Chettan who suddenly plunged into the water. After a few minutes, Padmanabhan surfaced carrying the still body of Kishore. I gazed at my dearest friend, his bulging stomach pressed against Padmanabhan's head—a proven method to expel water and mud embedded in his stomach and lungs. Despite all efforts to revive him, they proved futile. I never realized that I was looking at my close friend for the last time as I could not understand what was going on there or what ultimately happened to Kishore. Seeing the awed expression on my face, my wailing sisters forcibly took me inside and I never saw Kishore again. My friend, with whom I was laughing and playing just moments ago, was now lost to me forever. In the following few days, I was not allowed to leave my room. Amma tried to console me by saying that Kishore had gone up in the heavens to see the God, an explanation that did not satisfy my curiosity. Later, from the subdued talks of the elders, I understood that his body was taken to the hospital and later buried in the southern courtyard of his small house. After a few days, when I was allowed to go out, my playmates showed me the place where Kishore was laid to rest. There was a small mound of wet soil with a *Tulsi* plant and dried flowers scattered over it. Though I was hardly five when this happened, the untimely death of my childhood friend had left a deep wound in my heart. I vividly remember that in his final moments, he was wearing a blue trouser which he had kept in place by tying the loose ends together as they had no buttons. Even after all these years, the memories of that fateful day are etched permanently in my mind.

Rahim was the second child of Velikkakath Hamza and Pathumma, who belonged to a well-known middle-class family in our locality. He lived a carefree life surrounded by his parents, grandmother, uncles, aunts, and siblings in a large extended family. We were close friends and our homesteads were separated by a narrow strip of land that belonged to my aunt, Bhavani *Kunjamma*. They lived in a big tiled house of typical Kerala style and was located in the middle of a vast compound of more than an acre. The house had a veranda that wrapped around the building, with a small kitchen separated from the main building by a narrow corridor. The interior of the house was adorned with an array of ancient furniture, of which a *sapramancha kattil*, used by his *Ummumma* (grandmother), was a rare piece of furniture that was indeed a status symbol and a fine example of traditional Kerala carpentry. Beside the kitchen stood a tall Pamela tree (*Kumbulose Naranga*). His mother Pathumma, whom we affectionately called *Umma*, was a terrific cook and she used to serve us delicious *pathiri* and *irachikary* (mutton stew) on special occasions which we wolfed greedily. In the northeast corner, there was a pond, not very large but very deep. It was from this pond that water for all household needs was collected and people from the neighborhood also depended on it. Those were the days when resources like water, dried coconut spathe, fronds, and other parts of the coconut palm, which were used as firewood, were shared communally among the locals. It was a time when everything was shared, and nothing belonged exclusively to anyone.

Rahim was my bosom friend, a constant companion, and a playmate, though he was slightly older than me. Together we played many village games along with other friends, either in his sprawling compound or in the courtyard of my house. Games like police and thief and hide and seek were our favorite games in which girls also took part, though they were more interested in making *mannappam* with wet sand and applying henna on palms with a paste of henna leaves. With ease, they drew intricate designs on their palms. A huge tamarind tree stood in the southern corner and under its cool shade we played our games. With the house amid the vastness, the land was aplenty all around for us to play. During summer vacations, we would collect fallen, dried fronds of arecanut palms, known as *thanangu*, bundle them together in sets of three to four, and bury them in the courtyard. Later, on the eve of Vishu, we would burn them in a bonfire, a traditional ritual marking the beginning of the new year. We would also pick up fallen cashew nuts which would be roasted and their kernels would be used in the preparation of *Vishu kanji*.

During the summer vacation of 1969, I spent almost a month in the hospital with pneumonia and even after discharge, I was advised a month-long bed rest. During those days of isolation, Rahim would visit me along with his mother and enquire about my health. For me, leading a life isolated from my friends and classmates was unbearable. I spent time reading newspapers and textbooks which could alleviate my boredom to some extent. For me, days and weeks were uneventful and passed at a snail's pace. One evening while I was sitting in the veranda of my house, I was distracted by a hullabaloo and noisy talks from the direction where Rahim's house stood. The stillness of an otherwise calm and serene evening was broken as someone yelled at the top of her voice. Soon, I saw many men and women running towards his house. As I became curious, I informed my sister, Sheela, about the situation who at once joined the crowd and dashed to Velikkakath house. I too was keen to join them but Amma sternly refrained me from joining them. After a while, she too went out to ascertain the cause of the outcry. By now it was clear that loud wailing was coming from the house of Rahim, which unnerved me. After a few minutes, Amma came back, absolutely crestfallen with a flabbergasted expression and she hemmed and hawed initially but finally broke the unfortunate news that Rahim, while practicing swimming on his own, had drowned in the family pond. I suddenly felt my heart throbbing uncontrollably. With a shudder, I realized that my intimate friend Rahim had passed away. Amma told the neighbors that by the time his body was fished out, he was already dead. As in the case of Kishore, in Rahim's case too, I was not allowed to see his lifeless body, fearing for the possible trauma that could cause to me. The rest of the shocking incident I pieced together from the conversations of Amma with my sisters and the elderly women in the neighborhood. From their conversations, I reconstructed the incident thus: on the fateful evening Rahim, after the usual playtime with his friends, tried to practice swimming, which I knew he attempted before in our presence. Using an empty copper pot that he kept upside down as a float, he swam around the shallow water at the pond's perimeter, clinging to it. He successfully completed a few rounds, which gave him the confidence to swim to the middle of the pond. On his final attempt, when he reached the middle, the deepest part, the pot suddenly upturned, water gushed in, and it lost its buoyancy. The pot, with Rahim clinging to it, slowly sank. It took a few minutes for his family to notice his absence which proved fatal for him. Though a few people in the crowd tried to give artificial respiration, he was already dead. The body was shifted immediately to the nearby government hospital and it was released the next day after completing the formalities. When he drowned, Rahim's mother Pathumma was away at her ancestral home in Koovappadam where the body was taken, before cremation. Amma, along with all the neighbors, went to Koovappadam, a few miles away from where we stayed, to see his still body for the last time before it was buried in a nearby Mosque.

Nearly five decades have elapsed since the untimely and tragic passing of my two childhood friends. Yet, their memories persist, continuing to haunt me to this day.

41. The Curious Life of Kochumariam

Every village has its unsung heroes and heroines of lore who have played a role in the historical milieu of the village. This is the story of an ordinary, quiet, and unassuming woman who lived in our village, her name was Kochumariam. She lived a life marked by hectic activities, exemplifying hard work and sacrifice.

Kochumariam lived along with her husband and children in a tiny thatched house, no bigger than a hut, on a small plot of land surrounded by canals on two sides. A lake flowed through the western periphery of her homestead. The river, a vast repository of fishes and clams, flowed southward, gradually merging with the nearby Vembanad Lake, just a short distance from our home.

For Kochumariam, picking clams from the lakebed by hand and picking meat was the main avocation. The entire family depended on the meager income which she earned from selling the clam meat. John, her youngest son, who was almost my age, was a lamé boy and a school dropout.

Kochumariam had a set routine that had remained unchanged for years, a steadfast tradition she had followed faithfully. Every day, after the morning chores, she would set out for clam picking, mostly alone, but at times accompanied by a neighborhood woman. The clam picking is an arduous and time-consuming task, which she carried out by diving deep into the lake and picking live clams from the lakebed. The black, shining clams would be embedded in the lakebed. Each clam she picked would be soon deposited in a small earthen pot kept on her head. The whole process required a lot of skill and patience. We, the young boys living in the vicinity, would watch her extraordinarily superhuman activity with awe. On many occasions, her long underwater dive made us fearful as we imagined that she had drowned and we waited with bated breath until she surfaced with a handful of clams that she had painstakingly collected. A little after noon, she would emerge from the lake with her day's catch securely put in the pot. When emerged from the lake, she would be completely drenched in water with her wet clothes stuck to her body Her palm and fingers appeared wrinkled from prolonged exposure in water.

The rest of her dreary round of job would commence in the afternoon by 3. For the separation of meat from live clams, she employed a very crude method. Water would be boiled in a large aluminum vessel with a wide mouth, over a hearth fired by coconut shells and dried coconut husks. Into the boiling water, the live clams would be transferred and would be boiled for a few minutes. Once in boiling water, the shells would open wide, making meat separation easier. When boiled, a peculiar and attractive smell emanated from the boiled meat, which filled the surroundings, a smell which I relished much. After boiling, she would decant the hot water from the vessel and the still-hot shells would be transferred in small quantities into a wide-mouthed bamboo sieve which has openings all over with two handles on either side. The openings would be large enough to allow the meat to pass through but small enough to retain the empty shells.

Then, the bamboo basket with the boiled clams would be shaken vigorously, back and forth and the brisk shaking would separate the meat from the shells. The separated meat would fall through the sieve and would be collected in another vessel. After the meat was separated, the empty shells would be discarded in a corner of the backyard, where children would compete with village crows to scavenge for any remaining meat that had managed to escape Kochumariam's thorough processing. By now, evening would have fallen, and the neighbors would gather in front of her hut to buy freshly cooked clams, straight from the hearth. The price was 20 paise per *nazhi*, equivalent to 250-300 grams in modern metrics. A *nazhi*, a traditional measuring cylinder made from a hollow bamboo stem, was a common unit of measurement used in those days.

Once the local sales were completed, she would change into a clean dress and would carry the vessel containing clam on her head. With her head downcast, she would make her way to the Palluruthy market, a mile east of her home. She wore the traditional attire of Christian women in ancient Kerala: a white *mundu* with plaits hanging down from the back, a white *chatta* (a long blouse reaching up to her hips), and a white *naadan* (a shawl draped across her shoulders). This traditional ensemble was a hallmark of her cultural heritage. In those days, there was an evening market, called *anthichantha* at Palluruthy, selling fresh fish and vegetables, as back then, ice and freezing were nonexistent. By dusk, she would return home, sometimes with the leftover clam meat, after a day's sales. Kochumariam and many women like her toiled a lot, struggled, and suffered silently to make a living for themselves and their families. She never looked tired of doing the monotonous and tiresome job every day. Her face was calm and serene, devoid of expressions. She faced the vicissitudes in her life with fortitude, for she epitomized the survival instincts of many illiterate women like her. Despite back breaking job, she had led a life of perpetual indebtedness. It seemed she had forgotten to laugh, perhaps the innumerable trials and tribulations in life might have erased her soft emotions, but an occasional smile adored her lips reddened by chewing betel.

42. Prabhakaran and Thankappan: The Celebrated Village Musicians

Prabhakaran and Thankappan were brothers who lived in our village. Both were tall, slim, and dark-complexioned. According to the elders in the village, from a very young age, the duo mastered playing musical instruments, Prabhakaran played percussion instruments like drum and Tabla while his brother Thankappan famed himself for playing wind instruments like Clarinet and *Nadaswaram*. Occasions may vary from celebratory to mournful, it may be the festival of the local temples or church or some religious ceremonies or marriages and moods may vary from sober and mournful as in events like funeral processions or it could be enjoyable as in some cultural programs like Carnatic music. Whatever the occasion and what may be the mood of the masses, the brother duo was an indispensable part of all the happenings in the village. The duo played doleful dirge in their instruments when they led funeral processions of Catholics, which was quite moving. In the olden days it was not uncommon that when someone in a rich catholic family died, they would engage hired mourners, who would cry loudly accompanied by breast-beating. They rendered their "service" for a pittance. For the funeral service, the ensemble invariably consisted of a couple of drummers, a couple of buglers and clarinet players, complete with those playing cymbals. A short while before the beginning of the funeral procession, the band would play a soulful and monotonous tune twice within a space of a few minutes. This would be a reminder to the people around, who want to join the crowd, that the procession was about to start. This would be followed by the arrival of people hurriedly to attend the funeral service. The band playing the dirge moved at the forefront of the funeral procession, to be followed by the relatives and friends in that order, forming a beeline. The band would play *"samayamara radhathil njan swargayatra cheyyunnu* "(In the Chariot of time, I Travel to the Heaven) a heart-rendering dirge written by Rev. V Nagel, a German missionary. (Later in the Malayalam movie *Aranaazhika Neram*, this touching dirge has been included as a slightly modified version of Vayalar Rama Verma, being sung by P Suseela and P Leela). Finally, the coffin containing the dead person would be carried by a few men at the rear as the procession moved forward to the church through the narrow village paths. When Panchayat Road became a reality, a hand-pulled hearse took over the job of transporting the body.

Till the mid-eighties, singing bhajans to the accompaniment of various instruments, was a common practice among rich Hindus during the final rituals associated with funerals. On those occasions, Prabhakaran would play *Mridangam* and Thankappan Harmonium, while a few elders in the locality would sing bhajans in their harsh sound much to the annoyance of the bereaved family.

During the annual temple festivals, Prabhakaran had the privilege of accompanying several renowned Carnatic vocalists on the *Mridangam*, while Thankappan mesmerized audiences with his unique and masterful *Nadaswaram* playing. These brothers were the constant companions of all events in the society. They made a living from the paltry amount which they were rewarded with for their musical performances. They had an innate musicality they fostered and groomed over the years, on their own, to perfection. Even today, many years after their death, they come alive in the memory of the elders as unsung heroes who once made all the celebrations and festivities in the village lively, enchanting, and memorable. But in those days, there was hardly anyone who could appreciate their musical talents and encourage them on their musical journey. They truly deserved better treatment from society for making all social events colorful and entertaining.

43. *Chavittunaatakam:* The Exotic Dance-Drama of Kerala

It was during one December afternoon in the mid-sixties, that our neighbor Josy came to our house with the news that a *Chavittunaatakam* performance was going to be staged at the St. Joseph church, Chirackal, during the New Year. The church was located hardly a mile from our place. Though my three elder sisters have heard a lot about this unique art form of Kerala, they never had an opportunity to view a live show. They pleaded with Amma to go there to see the drama live which she agreed after the initial reluctance. Thus, it was decided that on New Year Eve, we would go to the church and watch the dance drama, which gladdened us. This was a rare treat for us, as we had the opportunity to watch a live *Chavittunaatakam* performance for the first time in our lives, a memory that dates back around five decades to when I was just six years old. The drama was scheduled to be staged in an open space near the church by the side of a lake. The news of the drama was circulated in the entire village and even neighboring localities well in advance by word of mouth and everyone was eagerly waiting for the day.

On the day the drama was to be played, we started early from our house, to occupy a vantage point from where we could watch the drama unhindered. The atmosphere was clam and cold and Amma wrapped a blanket around me as I had a mild cold. By the time we reached there, a crowd had already been gathered in front of the temporary stage. We occupied the veranda of a nearby house of Bappu, an acquaintance of Amma from where we had a clear view of the stage. Though the time announced earlier had passed by the drama had not yet started. As the time passed by, the audience became restive and the youngsters among them started hooting and howling, while the elders waited, though impatiently. Finally, almost two hours after the announced time, the drama began with a loud and thunderous background music. The drama was performed on an unusually long and wide makeshift platform, made of wooden planks, that were kept together side by side and there was a huge red-colored glittering front curtain. The stage could accommodate as many as 30 actors at a time. The most curious onlookers gathered by the stage entrance, where they could catch a glimpse of the actors entering and exiting. However, their attempts to sneak a peek at the stage were promptly discouraged by the program volunteers. Back then, our locality was not yet electrified and power was provided by a diesel generator which continuously emitted a thick cloud of dark smoke, while its roaring could be heard from afar. As the curtain finally went up, the spacious stage had been converted into a medieval landscape with colorful backdrop depicting the streets, and buildings to the minute. On the stage, there were half a dozen actors all attired in glittering costumes with colorful lights adding to the luster. As a prelude, there was a dance involving all characters in lively motion to the tune of the song which I remember was in Tamil. Though for *Chavittunaatakam* many musical instruments like *Chenda, Thamber,* and *Chengila* were used, Clarinet dominated all others as it would be played almost throughout the drama. The story developed through a song. Artists would sing as they enter the stage and it would be followed by the chorus. The songs start at a subdued pace, but the tempo gradually picks up finally reaching a crescendo to a frenetic pitch. As the song ended, all the actors together started the stomping, characterized by brisk quick and vigorous movements, true to the name of the dance. On that evening, the troupe enacted *Karalman Charitham*, a stage adaptation of a biblical story. Since the characters were mostly European kings or biblical characters, their costumes were shining, resembling Greek and Roman attire, complete with crown, specter, glittering ornaments, and warriors with swords and shields. A perfect blend of drama and dance, complemented with vibrant acrobatics, it is also called *"Christian Kathakali"* because of the obvious similarities. Unlike other art forms, the characters in *Chavittunaatakam* always wore boots or shoes which produced a thudding sound as they stomped vigorously. The eye-catching and flamboyant costumes, along with attractive light and sound effects, are the specialties of the drama that continued to surprise me. The drama had many fighting scenes using swords and shields which, they acted as realistic as possible, with weapons being used with dexterity. The whole drama was a classic whodunit. The songs would be mostly in Tamil sprinkled with some Malayalam. It showed that they had done their rehearsals assiduously. The *Chavittunaatakam* of olden days would last for two nights or more and each one would be a night-long affair. However, the modern versions have been compacted to a 3-hour duration. After an hour or so into the dance drama, I lost my initial euphoria and slowly fell asleep, unperturbed by the loud noise of the instruments and stomping. I couldn't recall exactly when we came back home after the drama. That was my first ever viewing of *Chavittunaatakam*, though later in my life I had the opportunity to enjoy the drama a few times. It's a traditional art form of the Catholics. Most of the stomping drama would be centered around biblical themes. In recent decades, deviating from the strictly traditional Christian or western themes, many have attempted stories from Indian history and folklore with enormous success. Thus,

Chavittunaatakam like Lord Ayyappa and Velu Thampy Dalawa came to life. Though a dying art form, *Chavittunaatakam* troupes are still active in places like Gothuruth, Ponjikkara, Vypeen, Fort Kochi, and Chellanam. It is the grandiose dreams of the actors in these places which has revived the art form.

In the mid-seventies, a group of *Chavittunaatakam* aficionados in our locality formed a troupe and embarked on a novel idea, to make a story based on Ramayana, in a way that would make it suitable to be adopted for the stomping dance. It was a brave attempt marked by sincerity and diligence in equal measure. And they did perform, after almost two years of hectic rehearsals. All of them were poor villagers, engaged in avocations like masonry, carpentry, tailoring, or doing some unskilled work. But all of them had one thing in common; a strong passion for the dance-drama which united them. The songs, unlike in the traditional dance-drama, were completely in Malayalam and the rehearsals were conducted on every Sunday morning. We, the children of the locality, would assemble at the home of painter Kochappan, where rehearsals were arranged in his courtyard. Though the story was experimental, it could connect well with the expectations of the audience. Anastasia, the white extremely charming woman, who had a dark past that she had buried long back, donned the role of Sita. I remember a tall, lean foreigner with long golden blonde hair, who came by a motorbike, as a regular visitor to the rehearsal. The *joie de vivre* that I experienced in the rustic countryside was unfathomable.

After long rehearsal, the Ramayanam *Chavittunaatakam* was staged in our place. The drama, though being performed by a bunch of amateur actors, and arranged on a shoestring budget, turned out to be an Avant-grade drama, with all the ingredients of a typical *Chavittunaatakam* and had won the appreciation of the audience. The audience was fascinated by the theatricality of the performance. Set in *thandawa* style the *Chavittunaatakam* has twelve basic *chuvadu*. Based on the nature of the characters fine and evil characters had different *chuvadus*. Unlike other professional troupes they never had another chance to perform in front of an audience, but they seemed contented with the once-in-a-lifetime performance.

"*Kattiyakkaran*" the Joker plays an important role in the drama, and he would perform with great fun and panache. His role was to entertain the audience with witty remarks and funny interpretations of serious dialogues. Whenever the *Aasaan* (the Master) calls him, he is supposed to perform and enjoys unbridled freedom to enter at any time during the show. With his crazy attire, snowy beards, and protruding teeth, his presence had always enthralled the audience. Kakki, a *Chavittunaatakam* artist from our locality, acted as the joker in all dramas, earning him the nickname 'Joker Kakki'. He, however, was a village goon, who was involved in many acts of violence, had a criminal past and the villagers were afraid of him. He was often hired by the landowners to settle scores with their tenants.

Stomping of the foot would be so powerful and vigorous that this often resulted in the breaking of the wooden planks of the platform and this has earned the nickname *thattupolippan*, which means stage breaker, for the drama. The dance-drama stood out by its opulent stage settings, an ornate and highly colorful dress embellished with glittering decorative sequins, liberal use of an array of blinding color lights and high decibel music which begins as a slow-paced solo to grow gradually in tempo finally to a crescendo of chorus.

It's believed that *Chavittunaatakam* had been introduced into the land by the Portuguese when they conquered Kochi. Gothuruth, a sleepy island near Kochi, is said to be the birthplace of the drama. Chinna Thamby Annavi, affectionately known as *Aasaan*, a thespian of Tamil origin, is considered the father of *Chavittunaatakam* who is believed to have written and directed *Karalman Charitham*. "*Chavittunaatakam- Oru Charitra Padanam*"

(*Chavittunaatakam*- A Historical Study), authored by Sabeena Rafi, is an authoritative document that traces the history, origin, and evolution of theatre. Shaji N Karun's critically acclaimed film *Kutty Srank* has exposed this art form to the Western world through the brilliant performance by celebrated actor Mammootty.

There are close similarities between Kathakali and *Chavittunaatakam*, both being traditional art forms of Kerala, the former a performing temple art and the latter a traditional art staged in churches. Both have songs which are an admixture of two different languages, while in Kathakali it is Sanskrit and Malayalam, in *Chavittunaatakam* it's Tamil and Malayalam. In both arts, a story is presented in an episode that lasts two or more nights. With the emergence of modern forms of dance and drama, *Chavittunaatakam* gradually lost its importance and the dying art survives in the contemporary world because of its inclusion as an item of competition in the School Youth Festival in Kerala which has provided the art form a new lease of life. *Chavittunaatakam*, a vibrant and culturally rich dance form, is a perfect and colorful fusion of acting, singing, dancing, and the steps of Kalarippayattu, the ancient martial art of Kerala. Today, this dying art form needs to be protected for future generations.

44. *Kodathy Ammavan*: The Judge, Jury and Executioner of an Ancient Family

Growing up in Kochi, I had the privilege of encountering numerous elders in our extended family, each with unique connections. Some were bound by strong familial ties, while others were more distantly related. Interestingly, some had obscure connections, yet they maintained warm and endearing relationships with everyone in the family. *Kodathy*, meaning 'the court', was the nickname of a person who resided in Amma's ancient *tharavad* (family home). We affectionately addressed him as *Kodathy Ammavan*, acknowledging his distant connection to our family through *Ammumma*, our maternal grandmother. My curiosity about his lineage led me to inquire with the family elders, and my eldest brother provided the answers. According to him, *Kodathy Ammavan* was the son of *Vallya Appuppan*, the elder brother of *Appuppan*, our maternal grandfather. After his parents passed away, he was taken in by *Ammumma* and raised in the *tharavad*. His name was Ayyachan and Amma respectfully addressed him as Ayyachan *Kochaangala*, which meant young brother, even though he was much older than her own brothers. *Kodathy*, I know, was a dark complexioned swelt figure with a thin frame. With his body stooping forward, he walked with difficulty. His sole attire was a white, shabby, discolored *thorthu mundu* that scarcely extended above his thin, bony shanks.

Elders in the family still cherish vivid memories of *Kodathy Ammavan* as a young family member of the *"koottukudumbam,"* the joint family. He lived a life of penury, while his better cousins led a life of ease and wealth. He was a chronic bachelor but had great affection and love for his family. He had great awe and respect for *Ammumma* whom he addressed as *"kaarnnothy"* which means matriarch. After the untimely death of *Appuppan* in a pandemic of smallpox several decades back, it was *Ammumma* who reigned on the whole family.

I was told that during his youthful years, he spent his nights atop the *maalika*, the loft of the old Pullyadath *tharavad*. He, in fact, shared the space in the wooden attic with a distant relative, who later went on to become an erudite professor.

In those days, in a joint family, it was not unusual that petty squabbles might erupt, usually among children and sometimes among the grownups too, over trivial issues. Often such quarrels might lead to heated exchanges with recriminations flying back and forth. On such occasions both the complainer and the complainant would approach *Kodathy* to intervene and suggest an amicable solution. He would listen patiently to both the warring parties and based on his assessment he would pass the judgment. Interestingly, everyone would accept his judgment unquestionably. He was thus the judge, jury and the executioner of the *tharavad* in his own right. It was such judgments which earned him the moniker *"Kodathy"* which subsequently replaced his original name Ayyachan. He had deep love and affection for his niblings and he enjoyed their company. During family reunions, he tried to enchant the children and smiled, revealing his tobacco-tainted teeth.

During the prime time of his life, he made a living by rolling beedis in which he was skillful. He had a tiny shop alongside the Waterland Road besides the crematorium from where he did his beedi business, along with some miscellaneous items like toffees. Occasionally, he had the habit of secretly making beedis (hand-rolled cigarettes) laced with ganja (cannabis) and smoking them, knowing that *Ammumma* would sternly disapprove of such behavior. He indulged in this habit clandestinely, aware that she would not tolerate such misdemeanors. My eldest brother once saw *Kodathy* being sternly scolded by *Ammumma* for hanging his wet loincloth to dry on a clothesline in plain sight of the women of the household, an act considered immodest and disrespectful.

He spent the sunset years of his life in abject poverty. He literally became orphaned after the death of *Ammumma* in the mid-seventies. When the old *tharavad* was demolished to build the present one, *Kodathy* lost forever his much-favored place of dwelling. In the new house he was allowed to live in the small room adjacent to the front veranda, which doubled up as the Pooja room of the family. Later, by the fag end of his life, he contracted TB and his constant bouts of coughing and his nasty habit of spitting phlegm all around irked the occupants of the new house. He was then shifted to a small, thatched shed which was in a dilapidated shape, no better than a shack, near the newly constructed house where he had spent his final days. When died he was cremated in the south-eastern corner of the homestead beneath the huge mango tree alongside the cattle shed following the family tradition. His funeral pyre was made in the same spot where *Ammumma* was cremated. The family arranged a dignified cremation for him, marked by an absence of the customary wailing and breast-beating, as there were no kin to mourn his passing.

45. From Postmaster to Healer: Anchal Master's Remarkable Odyssey

Anchal Master was an iconic person in his own time who occupied a pride of place in the history of our village. His sobriquet "Anchal Mash" was an honorific that he inherited from his career as a postmaster in the village post office in the early fifties. His forerunners in the profession came to be known as *Anchal ottakkaran*, the name obtained from their job as a postman who had to run the length and breadth of his specified territory, delivering letters and other postal articles to the addressees, which were very rare those days. The *Anchal ottakkaran* would be equipped with a long spear for self-protection from street dogs and a bell would be attached to it to announce his arrival. Anchal Mash, as he was affectionately called by the villagers, later metamorphosed himself as a homeopathic doctor after retirement. My memory of him is not as a postmaster but as a doctor. As a doctor, he was held in high esteem and commanded the respect and admiration of the entire village. He had unusual diagnostic skills which made him quite famous even in the neighboring localities. Amma reposed great faith in his treatment and she sought his treatment for me and my elder siblings as well. During my childhood years, Amma would take me to Anchal Mash for the treatment of asthma, which was a recurring health problem. Every time he would give a dose of his medicine which in normal course would last for three days. Once the initial dose is consumed, again he would review the patient. Even after two courses of his medication if the patient complains that the condition has not improved much, an enraged Anchal Mash would bluntly tell the patient that he had no medicine to treat his or her disease and to consult someone else. Fearing his wrath, the patient would tell him that his or her condition had improved even when there would be no significant improvement.

One day I developed a high fever accompanied by pain on one side of the abdomen. My urine looked dark yellow. Then I was hardly seven or eight. Amma asked me to collect some urine in a glass bottle into which she put a few grains of raw rice and kept it undisturbed for half an hour. Then she poured out the urine from the bottle and surprisingly the grains absorbed the color and appeared yellowish. At once she concluded that I had been afflicted with jaundice as it was a crude yet proven test for jaundice and decided to consult Anchal Mash. It was only midafternoon and he would be taking his afternoon nap at this time. Amma was quite apprehensive about my condition and decided to pay a visit to his home much earlier than his usual appointment time of 4 pm to try our luck.

When we reached there, his wife came out and Amma informed her about my suspected case of jaundice. She said that he never consulted anyone at this odd hour, yet responding to Amma's request she went inside but only to be returned soon to convey his order to come back after 4. At the appointed time we came back. He was a medium-built man with thick closely cut white hair and a round clean-shaven face with sparkling eyes. He would be always serious and carefully maintained a distance from his patients. I was afraid of him though I liked his sweet medicine. He was in a contemplative mood. But Amma explained my symptoms in great detail which he heard silently.

This was followed by a barrage of questions from him, the meaning or relevance of many of them I couldn't understand. Amma patiently and respectfully answered all his queries. Next, he would meticulously examine my eyes, then gently touch my forehead to check my temperature, and finally ask me to stick out my tongue, which I obediently did. It was an era when modern diagnostic equipment like thermometers, BP apparatuses, and Stethoscopes were nonexistent. The clinicians of those days relied on the time-tested diagnostic techniques involving *darsanam* (a close look at the patient); *sparsanam* (touching with bare hands on the forehead, chest and abdomen and then feeling the pulse by holding the wrist), and *chodyavali* (questionnaire) where the patient would be confronted with a barrage of questions which enabled them to diagnose the disease. I feel they did so, more by intuition rather than by measurement of parameters like pressure and temperature. After the routine checkup, he confirmed that I had jaundice, as Amma had feared and advised me to take four courses of medicine with a strict regimen of food- only liquid food without oil and salt was recommended for me till I fully recovered. I stood crestfallen and humbled as I knew for the coming fortnight, I would have to survive on *podiyari kanji* made of broken rice and *pappadam chuttathu*. For common childhood maladies, we would always allow the children to take a few pieces of crunchy rusk and *venna biscuits* (bun-shaped butter cookies) with *kattan chaya* but for me, this dietary choice was also denied much to my consternation. The very thought sickened me much more than the jaundice itself. However, I tried to hide my unpleasant feelings.

In hindsight, I realize the great services rendered by Anchal Mash as our village physician which he did more as a social service than for earning a living. As a child, I always liked visiting his house which, by the standards of those days, was quite large. He had a modest yet beautiful garden in his front yard with a wide variety of roses which he tended daily. Ducks quacked noisily as they walked among the bushes in search of food. Bordering the northern edge of his property lay a broad, shallow canal known as *vallaathu*, where flocks of ducks swam in joyful abandon. It was along these banks that the massive *kettu valloms* were moored.

Every day in the morning and evening he would consult his patients in his small, nondescript clinic at Palluruthy Veli. The clinic was indeed a small rectangular room, partitioned by a curtain, into two unequal sections. While the front portion was his consulting room where examined his patients, the rear section was used for storing medicines in a couple of wooden almirahs. It was here that he mixed medicines on a marble piece and dispensed into portions, each one covered by thin butter paper. As he mixed the medicines with a steel knife it produced a clattering. Interestingly, the front portion of the room he shared with a goldsmith (*thattaan*). Whenever I visited, I would gaze in wonder, my eyes wide with amazement, as the goldsmith skillfully placed tiny pieces of gold into a clay pot filled with rice husk (*umi*). He would then burn the rice husk, carefully positioning the gold on a small metal object, and gently blow on it using a small blowpipe, shaping it with precision. This was a sight to behold. The molten gold was then transformed into exquisite ornaments of his choice.

Anchal Mash led a life of affluence. His lifestyle spoke eloquently of his middle-class opulence. He was fastidious in his appearance. Resplendent in his impeccable attire, consisting of a spotless white *mundu* and a white Jubba adorned with gold cuff buttons, he cut a majestic figure. Always carrying a stylish umbrella with a curved wooden handle (*kalan kuda*), he exuded grandeur. His mode of transportation was a hand-pulled rickshaw, elegantly outfitted with a brass horn, a seat covered in rich red Rexine, and a lantern attached to the right handle, adding a touch of vintage charm. Every day he would travel in this rickshaw to the clinic and back which was located a mile away from where he lived. The rickshaw was pulled by Kakki, his faithful companion and driver and they journeyed through the village roads. The rickshaw was parked in a small shed in a place where the village road ended by the side of the *kaayal*. His house was located around 250 meters from where the rickshaw was parked and he had to walk through a narrow alley flanked by his paddy fields on one side and the narrow canal on the other.

The old tiled house at Palluruthy, where he lived happily with his family for several decades, had been demolished a few years ago to construct a new one for his youngest son. Thus, the old magnificent house and its illustrious occupant became a part of our collective memory.

46. Silent Valley: Expedition to a Precious Yet Vulnerable Evergreen Forest

In November 2022, my extended family of a couple of dozen people embarked on a trip to Silent Valley which lasted two days and a night. The mood was upbeat and the journey began with enthusiasm and fervor. Though we feared rain may play spoil sports with our plans, as it had been raining for the past few days and the weather forecast was also not favorable, we had a sunny and vibrant climate throughout our trip.

Much had been heard about Silent Valley since my high school days, when there was an ill-conceived move to construct a huge hydel power plant deep inside the virgin forest and subsequent agitations by environmentalists. The green brigade of the country came together under one umbrella and made "Save Silent Valley" a rallying point. Cutting across the political spectrum, the movement received great support and cooperation from different political parties, environmental groups, communal and social organizations. It was the largest ever successful environmental campaign which paved the way for a vibrant environmental movement in Kerala. Finally bowing to popular pressure, the government of the day had to abandon the project altogether for which the then Prime

Minister Mrs. Indira Gandhi played a key role. In 1984, the government declared this stretch of the rain forest as a national park to the relief of the people. Looking back, it's astonishing how the movement managed to garner widespread support from a significant portion of the population, considering the primitive state of communication technologies at the time. With only radio and newspapers as means of mass communication, the movement's ability to resonate with people across the country is a testament to its strength and appeal. Environmental evangelists like Prof. M K Prasad and Sugatha Kumari joined the bandwagon and led the movement. From then onwards I was aspiring to visit Silent Valley, one of the last remaining tracts of evergreen rainforests in India, which is a rich repository of several unique species of flora and fauna.

We reached the Inspection Bungalow of the Forest Department by evening and spent the night there, a completely silent night. Bhavani, one of the four east-flowing rivers of Kerala, had its origin a little ahead of where we stayed. The river originated as a small gurgling stream, laden with pebbles but further down, the stream broadened itself into a rivulet before ending up as a full flowing river whose banks crowded with overgrown thickets.

The next day, early in the morning we started our adventurous journey in three jeeps arranged by the Forest department. Our driver Mustafa, a young and handsome man, was a friendly and knowledgeable person. He doubled up as a tourist guide much to our delight and has all the attributes needed for a seasoned tourist guide. The road ahead was winding and overgrown with small plants, except for a narrow, concrete path about a foot wide, resembling a railway track. This solitary strip of concrete stood out amidst the lush vegetation, guiding us through the dense foliage. The width was hardly enough for a jeep to pass and no way to give side to another vehicle coming from the opposite side. To avoid such a situation the jeeps were allowed only in a single direction in groups of 10-15. After reaching the topmost point they return in a group the same way they ascended. These kind of tyre tracks ensures minimum destruction to the plants along the course. Along the way, he would stop now and then to explain about the rare plants and trees in the thick forest. At some point, in our arduous but refreshing journey through the hilly terrain, Mustafa slowed down the vehicle and pointed towards a human settlement nestled deep inside the forest. He explained that contrary to our long-held belief of tribals living in hutments in harmony with nature; here they live together as a community in small concrete structures, which had been gifted by the government as part of tribal development initiatives. But he hastens to add that it would have been better for them to dwell in their traditional ways in huts, as they used to be till recently, cheek by jowl in perfect harmony with nature. He lamented that the tribal development has indeed irreversibly altered the way they lived in peace and harmony.

Pointing to a paw mark and some still-drying excreta on the path, Mustafa said a tiger had passed by not long ago, maybe in the early morning. He said the valley is home to nine tigers as counted in the last wildlife census. He said the marks on their body are unique and that they are not similar for any two tigers, just like our fingerprints.

The forest is indeed a veritable cornucopia of several rare plants. *aanaviratty* is an innocuous-looking shrub but a deadly one that even elephants are scared of and hence the name. Once it comes in contact with the skin, Mustafa warned us, it would cause a burn-like skin irritation. On our ascending journey, he showed us *kaattu punna*, the timber of which was used for making the mast of sail ships in olden times. Another tree of considerable interest was the iron wood tree (*churuli*) whose Latin name is *Mesua nagassarium* which was used to make railway sleepers during the British period. At some point, Mustafa stopped his jeep along the roadside and showed us ferns with dark green color and much larger than normal leaves. He said these are very rare species of ferns much older than humans and millions of years ago these ferns were once savored by dinosaurs. This information aroused much interest in our group. Later I searched Google and found that he was right. The plant is indeed a giant tree fern (*Dinosaur pulpan*), a 50-million-year-old living fossil. The information was quite fascinating as we could see a fern whose ancestry dates back millions of years. This means that the forest we see today has undergone continuous evolution lasting millions of years. Along the way, he also showed us the wild varieties of arecanut, jackfruit tree, wild pepper, cardamom, and ginger. By the side of a sharp turn, we found a small wild stream, flowing down with a crackling sound. Mustafa stopped our vehicle and encouraged us to taste the pristine water. We all drank the water, and it had a unique, unfamiliar taste that was unlike anything we had ever experienced before. The youngsters in the group were engaged in photo shoots while I enjoyed the scenic views of the mountains. He enlightened us with the information that the British axed and removed valuable trees like ironwood tree and later exported them to their native land. A part of this virgin forest had been cleared for the cultivation of plantation trees, mainly eucalyptus and acacia for the paper industry and also teak. As he drove forward through the forest, Mustafa explained that the rain forest has several distinct layers such as forest floor, herb layer, shrub layer, understory, canopy, and emergent. He further told us that each layer has its own unique plant and animal species that interact with each other.

As we moved up white clouds floated freely in the clear blue sky like bits and pieces of cotton which was breathtaking. When we arrived at the top, Mustafa's face lit up and he talked excitedly about the landscape and its varied forms of life.

From the point we alighted from our jeep the one-hundred-foot-tall fire watch tower appeared in silhouette against the backdrop of the vast blue sky. In the scenic natural surroundings of the forest, the mammoth steel structure appeared incongruous. I stood atop the tower braving the gusty, cold wind and enjoying the picturesque landscape. The sound of the strong breeze resonated in the forest wilderness. The view of the valley from atop the watch tower left me flabbergasted. I had a panoramic view of the Sairandhri Vanam with Kuntipuzha meandering through the mountain slopes far-away. The view of Silent Valley from afar was breathtakingly beautiful, decorated with bright red flowers of *Butea frondosa*, "the flame of the forest" (*chamatha* in Malayalam) which was in full bloom- a sight to behold. Mustafa told us that in Mahabharata the Pandavas spent their years of *vana vaasa*, (exile in the forest), in this dense forest, and hence the name *Sairandhri Vanam* (Sairandhri is the pseudonym assumed by Draupadi during her life in hiding). Names such as Kuntipuzha and Paatrakkadavu are also related to the epic. He said it was at Paatrakkadavu that Kunti washed the *Akshaya patra*, the inexhaustible vessel. I was impressed by his vast knowledge of epics, combined with his passionate dedication to nature conservation and environmental protection.

The salubrious climate and lush green landscape together provided an ethereal atmosphere. Gradually the winter wind gained strength and turned chilly. We walked cautiously through the grasslands as we feared the blood-sucking leeches which are too many. The serenity and tranquility of the atmosphere transcended me to another world. I told myself that I was looking at an ancient rainforest much older than the human race, where dinosaurs might have once roamed freely in gleeful delight. The very thought gave me goosebumps. Once again, I reminded myself that this patch of evergreen forest is the only one of its kind still surviving and we are duty-bound to preserve and protect this forest for our future generations. The virgin forest of Silent Valley, which forms part of the Nilgiri hills, is home to a variety of rare and unique flora and fauna many of which are labelled as "critically endangered" by the International Union for Conservation of Nature (IUCN). It was Dr Robert Wright, a Scottish Botanist who in 1847 named it Silent Valley because of the complete absence of cicadas. After spending an hour and a half, we returned slowly to the IB. Mustafa appeared disturbed when he said that climate change has impacted the Silent Valley forests too as cicadas are spotted in some places. The fragile ecosystem is a world in itself at risk of being destroyed my human interventions.

As we bid farewell to the last remaining patch of tropical rainforest and boarded our vehicle for the return journey, I silently expressed my gratitude to Walter Mendez, the creative director of Mudra Communications, an advertising agency, for endowing Kerala with the captivating sobriquet "God's own country". This iconic tagline, coined by Mendez in 1989 for Kerala Tourism, has become an enduring testament to the state's natural beauty and allure.

47. On Greetings Cards

Recently as I was digging through my bookshelf, I had a chance to discover a few old greeting cards. Those were indeed fascinating colorful cards of the early nineties which I had sent from Nairobi, the capital of Kenya where I worked for a brief time in 1992. Almost all of them splendidly pictured the breathtakingly gorgeous landscape of the East African country.

Those who were born before the seventies have fond recollections of Christmas cards which were once available in a multitude of colors and patterns. While a vast majority of them depicted beautiful paintings of contexts from the Bible, mostly the birth of Jesus Christ in Bethlehem. During my school days, Christmas and New Year were two eagerly awaited occasions for receiving greeting cards from my two brothers and cousins. The impatient waiting for the arrival of the postman bringing those priceless cards would begin a few days ahead of Christmas. It was a once-in-a-year occasion when a postman would bring envelopes addressed to me which would be a profoundly comforting experience for me. After my persistent request for many days, Amma would at last give a meagre amount using which my sister and I would buy Christmas cards and send them to a couple of friends and close relatives. In the late sixties and the seventies, such cards were not so common and would be available only in a few shops in the village. When dispatched as "Book Post," only 20 paise adhesive stamps were required for a card but the envelope could not be sealed and should be kept open by simply inserting the open flap into the envelope. An envelope fully sealed would attract stamps of higher value and naturally, we preferred the former. We, however, received such greeting cards in sealed envelopes.

Back then, we used to collect old Christmas cards which would be displayed along with the festive decorations in the crib. I had a magnificent collection of old greeting cards, though most of them were lost irretrievably during packing and shifting of residence twice. In those happy old days, our joy knew no bounds as we received a hand-delivered card from the postman. On many occasions out of curiosity, we would ask him if we had any cards. He would say that if anything was there, he would safely deliver it at our doorstep. He was a tall man with a receding hairline and was overly friendly.

The greeting cards expressed a range of emotions like love, joy, gratitude, camaraderie, adulation, sentiments, and a lot more. There used to be an invisible emotional connection between the sender and the recipient. The imagery was as captivating as the messages. I used to keep all old Christmas cards as a memento of a hilarious time. Nowadays we send greeting cards on many occasions like marriage, birthdays, wedding anniversaries, Father's Day, Mother's Day and to commemorate special occasions like Onam, Diwali, and Pooja but back then greeting cards were sent only for Christmas and New Year.

However, by 2010 the traditional practice of sending Christmas and New Year cards have been replaced by e-cards and social media posts. This kind of greetings, most of which are forwarded messages, has taken away much of the charm and warmth of exchanging printed paper cards. In this era of digitalization, cards are often being sent through digital devices even for trivial reasons like baby showers, pet's birthdays and all and they lack the love, joy, and emotionality of the greeting cards of the past decades. Greeting cards are tools using which we connect psychologically and emotionally with our near and dear ones.

Till a few years ago I made it a practice to send birthday cards to all staff and colleagues in the company where I worked as CEO. My secretary would remind the birthday of each staff member a couple of days before the date and she would send a custom-made card with the company logo and a wonderful birthday message signed by the MD of our company and beside myself so that on the birthday he or she would receive it. The small act of compassion had a profound impact in boosting the employee morale as they realized that the company management cares for them.

HISTORY OF CHRISTMAS CARDS.

Christmas card has a fascinating history that dates back to 1843 in Britain. It was around this time that the British Post introduced the ambitious "Penny Post" which enabled people to send posts anywhere in Britain by affixing a penny stamp, which became hugely popular. Sir Henry Cole, best remembered as the founder of the Victoria and Albert Museum in London, had a wide friendship circle and all of them used to send greeting letters to him on Christmas via the "Penny Post". He was overwhelmed by the sheer number of such letters received and since it was considered impolite not to reciprocate and for Victorians responding to a letter was a social obligation, he was in a dilemma. Finally, he found an innovative way, he sketched an imagery of a family celebrating a toast with a simple message underneath which read "A Merry Christmas and Happy New Year to You". He got this printed and sent it to all his friends and thus fulfilled his social obligation. In the olden days, Christmas and New Year cards served to reunite and sustain familial bonding and friendships.

In Christmas cards that we sent to our brothers, we used to scribble short messages on the reverse side of the cards. People with a penchant for art used to make fantastic homemade cards.

Today the noble gesture of exchanging Christmas cards among the near and dear ones is on the wane. Instead, cards created by digital devices are becoming a norm. In this digital era of instant messaging is there a future for old greeting cards sent by snail mail? Highly unlikely.

48. Monsoon Magic of Bygone Decades

As I pen this article on this mid-June evening of 2023, a relentless rain has been pouring down on my city for hours, casting a soggy spell over the night. Indeed, it has been raining cats and dogs, so vigorously that most of west Kochi is flooded. It is raining ferociously as if to make amends for the delayed onset contrary to the normal date of June 1. South west monsoon is lashing Kerala in full fury, which was accentuated by a hurricane.

Like most children of my generation, I loved and cherished the arrival of the monsoon. Torrential rains filled us with childlike exuberance, though continuous rain would play spoil sport with the working class. Those rainy days were filled with pure delight.

In our cultural milieu rain occupies an important place, a much-awaited guest whom we welcome with gusto. Where else the rain is welcomed with such enthusiasm and fervor as in our culture? We used to greet the first rain of the season by singing the welcome song *"mazha vaaa….., mazha vaaa…,, mazhakku chakkara peera tharaam"* as we walked along, lapped up, loosely translated as "come rain, come rain, we will give you sweet jaggery and coconut mix". It was a poetic way of inviting rain and expressing a desire for the sweet joy that rain brings.

Whereas in temperate European culture rain is viewed as an inconvenience and seldom gets the kind of acceptance and welcome we give. In the European culture the children try to drive away the rain by singing

"Rain, rain, go away

Come again another day

Little Tomy wants to play ".

While our children welcome rain by offering their choicest titbits, their western friends try to drive away the rain by asking angrily to come later: two entirely different cultures with different outlooks.

The first rain has brought about a cool and refreshing feeling which has quenched the thirst of the parched soil and a peculiarly enjoyable smell, the petrichor as it is called, emanated from the wet soil. Rain has an uncanny ability to change our mood from dull and emotional to that of sober and thoughtful. Who doesn't love to sit on a couch, sipping hot tea and watching the enchanting beauty of the rain? Kerala indeed is the gateway of Indian monsoon as the state receives the first spell of rain in the subcontinent in the first week of June. From here, the rain slowly progresses northward covering the entire country within a fortnight. The nightfall after the first few rains would be particularly miserable as moths would appear from nowhere and would conquer the entire area in their thousands much to the discomfiture of the people. But they are short-lived creatures and attracted by the flames of the kerosene lamps, they fly together toward the light and soon perish- harbingers of a new rainy season. Then Pussy and Chaky, our pet cats, had a field day (or night?) as they savored a hearty dinner.

Ours is an agrarian economy, agriculture being the prime mover of our economy, which in turn depends heavily on the vagaries of the climate. A normal rainfall at the right time is all we need to buoy up our economy to new heights. Whereas deficient or excessive rains are equally dangerous as they can spell disasters for the agricultural sector.

The deluge which we have experienced in recent years has, however, changed the outlook of many. Today many in Kerala view rain as an inevitable inconvenience that can affect lives and property. These days people welcome rain not with enthusiasm and cheerfulness as they used to be but with a sense of fear and trepidation. As the thick clouds gather overhead and the sky becomes overcast, many shudder. The very thought of the 2018 flood is unnerving and sends shock waves.

In the past, we had vast areas of agricultural lands, rivers, rivulets, canals, ponds, and open fields which served as reservoirs, and floods were controlled to a great extent by them.

After a few days of incessant rains during *edavapathy*, in June-July months, the vast school playground, which was the size of almost five football fields, would soon be turned into a rivulet. Delightfully we would wade through knee-deep water, precariously balancing the school bag and umbrella in our hands braving heavy gusts. It provided a mischievous occasion for grown-up boys as they splashed the stagnant water with their bare feet making loud noises which they enjoyed. The younger boys would derive pleasure by throwing small, flat pieces of broken earthen pots which would glide over the surface of water.

After several days of relentless rain, there would occasionally come those precious moments where sunlight pierced through the showers. In those moments, we would burst into song, chanting *'veyilum mazhayum, kaattile kurukkante kalyanam.'* This phrase, which translates to 'sunshine and rain unite, marking the fox's wedding in the woods,' is an expression which encapsulates the fancifulness of this natural spectacle. A similar saying in English, 'the devil is beating his wife,' also refers to this phenomenon of "sun showers". To us children, the rarity of "sunny rain" was nothing short of magical.

Back then most students including my classmates did not have an umbrella of their own and they covered themselves with a leaf of taro or plantain leaves. Those who had an umbrella shared with their friends. When I was admitted to first standard Amma gifted me a colorful umbrella made of thick cloth of red, blue, green, and yellow and a wooden shank with an attractive plastic handle. When water drops fell on the surface of the umbrella it produced a particular tick tick sound which I liked very much and as the cloth wets the sound would change from harsh to somewhat softer. I seldom shared my umbrella with anyone else. Whether shine or rain I always carried my umbrella which indeed was an inseparable part of my identity.

Once during a rainstorm in the afternoon, I was going to my sister's class who was then in high school. It was raining unusually heavily with strong gusty winds. Suddenly there was a minor cyclonic storm and I was caught in the eye of the storm. While all the others ran for safety to the nearest school veranda, I continued walking with my umbrella open, it acted like a parachute and I was lifted a few feet off the ground. Seeing my predicament some teachers and senior students who huddled in the school veranda called out in loud noise to abandon my umbrella. I, instead, held it even more tightly. Fortunately, the storm lasted only for a few seconds and then it vanished throwing me onto the ground underneath the huge peepal tree where I landed with a thud. Ever since, wind has become a constant source of utmost fear for me and made me an anemophobic for the rest of my life as I have an eerie feeling whenever a heavy wind blows especially accompanied by rain. This, however, did not dampen my love for rain and I remain a staunch and real pluviophile, one who loves rain. The torrential rains rekindled memories of our childhood days when we played in puddles and flooded courtyards by floating paper boats in just dandy. Rain produces a multitude of sounds depending on the intensity of rain and the kind of surface where it falls which is called a "pitter patter"

Recent decades have witnessed a drastic change like monsoon in Kerala and has become unpredictable. This may be due to the effects of climate change and related events like cloud bursts and very heavy rainfall accompanied by cyclonic storms have become common occurrences. Kerala, however, has learnt to survive with resilience. The monsoon not only replenish the dried-up water bodies and nourish the greenery but also satiate the soul and culture of the people.

49. The Crazy World of Anthappan

Anthappan along with his wife and only daughter Philomina whom everyone called Philo, lived in a small two-room brick walled house with tiled roof near the southern side of our homestead. The two compounds were separated by a fence made of palm leaves. He has been a lunatic for as long as I can remember. He would not do any work and used to spend his day in his imagined world of hallucinations. His meagre possessions included a wooden cot, a bench, and a few household items like earthen pots and aluminum vessels. He would often sit on the bench kept in the small veranda for most of the day merely talking to himself. His soliloquies were an almost inaudible whispering. We, the children of the locality, were much afraid of him though he never, not even once, scolded or rebuked us. He seemed to be living in a phantasmagorical world and we silently enjoyed his eccentricities and mannerisms from our side of the fence through a peephole we made for the purpose.

On Saturdays, he would go out seeking charity from a few wealthy families in the village which he visited regularly but he seldom sought any contributions from others, unlike ordinary mendicants. Those who he approached knew him well and they paid him generously. When went out, he always dressed himself in a white *mundu* which would be folded above his knees, a white shirt and a shawl (*naadan*) over his shoulder, and a small cloth bag hanging on his hand. When Achan came for his annual leave, he would gift Anthappan a few packets of cigarettes much to his delight.

Elders in the village recalled that years ago he was a skilled worker in making the "*vadom*" also called "*aalaath kayar*" which are unusually thick cables of coir ropes made by coiling several strands of ropes. The *kayar* rope is valued for its strength, durability and long life. Making *aalaath kayar* called "*aalaath piri*" was a skillful and laborious exercise in which he excelled. In those days such coir cables were in great demand and were widely used for tying boats and fishing craft and also for supporting huge trees from falling on nearby objects while cutting them down. Back then it was a highly paid job and he was leading a life of contentment with his family. But fate had something else for him and slowly he started showing signs of mental illness. Gradually he stopped working altogether in a yard at Mattancherry and instead engrossed himself in a world of his own, quite oblivious of the realities around him.

Once on a fine morning, much to the amusement of the villagers, he appointed himself as the "President of India" which he declared in an important speech that he delivered from the veranda of his house. The children were fascinated by the quirky behavior of Anthappan. Though his wife scolded him using the choicest insults, he was undeterred and decided to continue in his newfound role as the first citizen of the country.

A few days later, much to our surprise, he fixed a wooden board painted blue in which it was written in white Malayalam letters "A.A. ANTHAPPAN, INDIAN PRESIDENT".

Interestingly he took over the presidential responsibilities at a critical phase in Indian politics, that was during the emergency, when Fakruddin Ali Ahmed was the President. The news of Anthappan becoming the President after dethroning Fakruddin

Ali Ahmed amused the village people. A few days later when he called Achan and said now onwards no one would be allowed to conduct marriages and defaulters would be punished. In those days Achan was trying to fix the marriage of my elder sister. He said, "No Anthappan, till we get your nod I won't arrange a marriage", Achan assured him which seemed to satisfy him. Soon his "popularity" increased and whenever we mentioned the location of our house to someone, he/ she would mockingly remark that adjacent to the house of the Indian President.

On important occasions like Independence Day and Republic Day, he would hoist the tricolor in his courtyard on a slender wooden pole. Standing on the veranda and facing the open courtyard, he delivered passionate political speeches as if addressing a large crowd. He spoke eloquently on many important topics and in one such address he dealt at length about joblessness among the youth. While his quirks delighted the children, the grown-ups silently enjoyed his funny and whimsical orations. The Malayalam adage which translates as "it's fun to watch when someone's mother goes crazy" applied to the collective behavior of the villagers. When his madness seemingly became intense, he was subjected to shock treatment that his frail body could not tolerate. He died in the early eighties. While looking back, it is with a sense of pain and sorrow, I recollect the life of a poor man who lived in a fanciful world of his, quite oblivious of the happening around him, not even perturbed by the hardships of his own family. Even now society's attitude toward people with mental illnesses has not changed much.

50. Amma and Her Culinary Excellence

Amma was an excellent cook with marvelous culinary skills and during her youthful years, she used to make a variety of traditional dishes. She had spent a considerable part of her life in the kitchen preparing various types of food for the family which she always shared with children in our neighborhood.

We had a small, tiled, nondescript kitchen attached to the main building of the house which had two unusually wide and tall grilled windows. Those were the days when many of the modern amenities that we enjoy today like potable water, cooking gas, and electricity were conspicuously absent. There was a hand pump from which we drew ground water for washing clothes and utensils while for cooking drinking water supplied by the Municipality was used. My elder siblings were tasked with the collection of water from a tap located in a faraway area in copper pots. This was indeed an ordeal for them as they had to often fight with the clamoring village women in the locality. But they did their job uncomplainingly. Later Amma tasked a neighboring woman with collecting fresh water for which she had been given a reasonable remuneration. The eastern part of the long kitchen had been used as the cooking area where there were two hearths made of brick and mortar which had small pits at the bottom for placing the firewood and also to collect the ashes. The other end of the kitchen doubled as the dining area where a small wooden desk with half a dozen wooden stools was placed. Every day in the early morning it was an arduous task for her to bring the fire to life by blowing continuously with a blowpipe. By the time the hearth was aglow with the fire burning in full force, the entire kitchen would be filled with smoke and soot which would suffocate Amma and she would cough hard. During wet rainy days, she had to struggle even harder to fire the hearth. This apart, we also had a kerosene stove and a *kutti aduppu* which used sawdust as fuel. Just above the hearth, at eye level, there had been a wooden loft over which raw tamarind and small fishes would be kept for drying during rainy days.

Amma was an excellent cook with unmatched skills. Her paraphernalia included a couple of large copper pots (*chembu*) for cooking rice, another large wide-mouthed copper vessel for draining the cooked rice, several clay *chatty*, and *kalam* of varying sizes with matching lids, each for cooking a particular meal. Her kitchen wares also included a *Cheena chatty* (frying pan), and an assortment of *kayil* (spoons) made of coconut shells with long handles made of bamboo reeds. A few years later, a magnificent collection of copper wares like a large and one medium-sized *chembu*, a medium size *uruli*, half a dozen *kinnam* (brass plates) a copper kettle, and a few stainless-steel plates, and a few glass and steel tumblers were added to the list of appliances. Much later Achan brought a wooden rolling board and a rolling pin using which she initially made unusually thick and irregularly shaped chapathys. Later following the guidance of Achan, she mastered the expertise in the making of thin full moon-shaped chapathy.

Amma used separate utensils to cook different dishes like fish curry, mutton curry, and vegetable dishes. A special *kalam* was dedicated to preparing mutton soup which she prepared for Achan. During the month of *Karkkidakam*, she prepared *marunnu kanji*, the medicinal potion, for which another large *kalam* was earmarked which after use would be kept safely.

All newly acquired clay utensils would be subjected to a curing process by heating them in open fire while their interior would be fired with *umikkari*, the rice husk. This process would expose both the inside and outside of the culinary tools of clay to high temperatures, a process called *"mayakkal"* a kind of tempering. It was believed that this kind of heat curing would enhance the strength and longevity of the kitchen wares.

Back then all ingredients such as chili, turmeric, coriander, pepper, and the like would be ground in a granite mortar (*ural*) using a long wooden pestle with metallic heads on either side (*ulakka*). It indeed was a cumbersome task. During festivals and on special occasions, when a large volume needed to be ground, my two elder sisters used to grind as a team with each one striking the pestle alternating in quick succession. Coconut and coconut oil were liberally used as universal ingredients for the preparation of both vegetarian and non-vegetarian dishes.

Amma was a culinary expert which she learnt partly from *Ammumma* and rest from her own experience. Her Fish Molly made of *Karimeen* (pearl spot) was quite popular among our relatives and friends. So was the mutton curry which she prepared with potatoes. On special occasions and when guests were invited for lunch, as a rule, she would serve Puri and mutton curry as starters. This would be followed by a lavish meal of *Karimeen pollichathu, meen curry, moru kaachiyathu, aviyal* and *mezhukkupuratty,* and *pappadam.* Occasionally when crabs were available, she would make *varutharacha njandu curry* with pieces of raw banana which had tongue tinkling taste. Another unique dish that she had made was *chemmeen ularthiyathu* with pieces of *karikku,* (sautéed shrimp with tender coconut) together they made an amazing dish. *Chemmeen vada* (prawn cutlet); fried clam meat, *meen peerapatichathu* are all some of her favorite non-vegetarian gourmets. Prawn pickle made of fried prawns in vinegar was one of her splendiferous preparations. Along with most vegetarian dishes like raw banana, *achinga* (long bean), *amara payer* (broad bean), *cheera* (spinach), and beans she liberally used small-sized peeled shrimp as an ingredient which enhanced the taste and flavor of the curry. Quite infrequently she used to prepare a rare kind of curry, fried *chemmeen parippu*, the dried prawn pulp, which had an extraordinary flavor that we munched excitedly, was indeed a delectable preparation. During the season of oil sardines, Amma would separate the fat from the fish and would be used to prepare *appam* of wheat flour fortified with the fish oil which had many health benefits.

She would use all available vegetables, including their flowers and tender leaves in her modest kitchen garden where she had cultivated snake gourd and bitter gourd which would be spread over the horizontally raised trellis of coir while spinach would be planted underneath. A stone would be tied to the end of the snake gourd and bitter gourd to ensure that they grow straight and elongated. Her preparation of a *mezhukkupuratty* using the tender leaves and flowers of yellow pumpkin with lentils tasted superb. She would also make *thoran* using the *vaazha pindy*, the soft stem of plantains, and *vaazhakudappan;* banana bunch.

During summer months she would buy *Pallathy*, (the spotted etroplus), the little cousin of *Karimeen* which were abundantly available then and they would be dressed, smeared with a paste of masala, and dried. During rainy days, when there would be no fresh fish, she would fry the dried *Pallathy* which had a mouthwatering flavor. During lean months when no fish were available, she would prepare *unakka chemmeen chammanthy*, the chutney made from dried shrimp which was a gastronomic delight. Beef was conspicuously absent from her menu which she never allowed to cook in our house owing to religious sentiments.

For breakfast, we usually had light dishes like *Puttu* and *Kadalakkari*. *Pazham* or *Pappadam*, *Upma*, *Maniputtu* or *Dosa*.

For evening tea several finger foods would be available such as *Kozhukkatta* (sweet dumplings), *pidi* (rice dumplings); *Achappam*, *avalose Podi* or *Avalose unda*.

It was during the preparation of the *Ona sadya*, that her culinary skills would be put to the ultimate test. During my childhood years she single-handedly prepared the elaborate *sadya* with 12-14 different items including *inchycurry, ullicurry, sambar, rasam, aviyal,* and *payasam*. She had a specialty dish made of peeled shallots and sliced green chili. The curry though too hot and spicy, was tremendously tasty. She had shared the rare recipe for this dish with my eldest sister. Though Amma did not have a recipe book, she could remember the recipe of each dish by heart. All the different ingredients were used by the rule of thumb in the absence of a standardized recipe.

In the fifties and sixties most of our neighbors led a penurious life and, on many days, they would be forced to starve. Amma was benevolent enough to feed many of my neighborhood friends. Once my close friend and neighbor Robert's thatched house was completely gutted in a devastating fire when we were hardly five. Amma used to feed him and his elder brothers, George and Josy for days together which they used to recall fondly later in their life.

Later by the fag end of her life, gas stove, mixer-grinder, fridge, and other such modern appliances became available. But she still preferred to mix the ingredients on the grinding stone and to cook her favorite fish and mutton curry in the traditional *aduppu* as she believed the food would not be that tasty when a mixer and gas stove were used. Her conclusion was right indeed as such foods cooked traditionally tasted better.

The food which Amma served had the flavor of human love and the taste of human kindness. In her death, we lost a repository of culinary secrets as she did not leave a documented recipe for us to follow her culinary tradition.

51. The Tale of a "Crime" and "the Punishment"

Every village has its tragic heroes with an incredible tale to tell. Many such stories fed to us vary from mere gossips to manufactured lies and exaggerated realities. The one that is narrated here belongs to the last category maybe with a little bit of exaggeration. Chaury was an ordinary mortal of our village who had led an ordinary life. He had nothing special about his life to make him a subject of my narrative.

He lived a happy life in the company of his caring wife and adorable children in a small thatched house in our village. He had died many decades ago. I came to know about his life story through the gossip of the village elders. He was leading a contended life until one day fate had upturned his life. One day a small gold ornament was ostensibly stolen from a nearby house of Chaury. An arduous search for the missing chain proved unsuccessful and the family of the stolen article approached the local police station. As part of their investigation to collect evidence, the police questioned the woman whose ornament had been stolen. She was subjected to an extensive interrogation by the police, who repeatedly asked her if she had any suspicions about the theft. Although she initially denied having any suspects in mind, she eventually hinted to the police that she had seen Chaury in the area shortly before the theft was discovered. Without wasting time, the police immediately took him into custody and took him to the station where he was questioned. During the interrogation, Chaury pleaded his innocence. But the police concluded that he was the culprit and framed him in the theft case.

The news spread quickly in the village and soon it became the talking point among the villagers. In a fraction of a second, he felt his life turning upside down. The villagers immediately awarded him the derogatory prefix *"Kallan"*, a thief, that moment witnessed the sudden transformation of Chaury the gentleman to Chaury the thief. After registering an FIR, he was released on bail. However, a few days later the police arrested another man in connection with another case of robbery. Quite fortunately for Chaury, during his questioning, the thief admitted that it was he who stole the gold ornament that was put on the head of Chaury. Thus, by the ironic twist, Chaury could prove his innocence to the law enforcement officers though the disgraceful title *Kallan* became a permanent fixture of his name. He was destined to lead the rest of his life as *Kallan Chaury* though everyone knew that he was indeed innocent. This is exemplified by the fact that when he died, he was given a church burial befitting any God-fearing Catholic. In those days people like thieves, antisocial people, atheists, and communists were denied a decent church service and instead, they were buried outside the cemetery called *"themmadi kuzhi"* which means "rouge's pit". After his death, his wife and children inherited the disparaging title *"Kallan"* which was passed down generations. The present generation of his family is, however, spared the stigmatization which their great-grandfather was made to suffer for no fault of his.

Thus, the story of *Kallan* Chaury is the heart-wrenching tale of a young man who was wrongly accused of a crime that he had never committed and the incident shattered the lives of his family. Many events, good or bad, which happen in our lives can change our lives forever. We are all slaves of the circumstances. Chaury's life reveals the incredible fragility and vulnerability of human life.

52. Fort Kochi: The Land where History, Culture, Traditions and Memories Coexist

The twin towns of Fort Kochi and Mattancherry have found a place on the world tourism map as must-see destinations in India. Fort Kochi is a fabulous place, a unique landscape that is an exquisite blend of culture, history, tradition, and memories. Whenever one thinks of Fort Kochi, the first image that comes to mind is that of the legendary Chinese fishing nets that line up the beaches at Kamaala Kadavu. The operation of the nets is a great tourist attraction, though many old nets have either been abandoned or demolished. It is believed that the fishing nets have been introduced to Kochi by the Chinese in the 14th century. With its neatly designed roads, beautiful pavements lined with several centuries old rain trees, attractive promenades, huge Chinese fishing nets, long beaches, magnificent mansions, historical buildings, and colonial architecture this ancient town is a heritage site. Fort Kochi is an ancient town frozen in time and space which lends it the old-world charm and calmness of a medieval town. Unsurprisingly, today the town is a much sought-after tourist attraction in India and abroad. As it closely resembles an old European town, people from far and wide throng the place attracted by its enchanting surroundings, unmatched natural beauty, cool and invigorating atmosphere, and serenity which make the town quite apart from other popular tourist destinations. I have always been fascinated by the scenic beauty and serenity of the town and during my college days in the late seventies at the nearby Cochin College, we used to frequent the place whenever we had free time. We used to spend long hours on the beach munching peanuts and cracking harmless jokes. Here life is slow-paced and calm, away from the maddening crowds of the city. When I stayed in Goa for a few months in the mid-eighties I was awestruck by the close similarities of Panaji with Fort Kochi. Both share a colonial past being conquered and ruled by the Portuguese and many of the awesome and imposing structures are the relics of the Portuguese era.

The history of Fort Kochi is unique in that this ancient land located at the far end of west Kochi had been conquered successively by three colonial powers such as the Portuguese, the Dutch, and the British in that order, leaving behind the indelible imprints of their cultural heritage. The Maharaja of Kochi permitted the Portuguese to build a fort at Kochi which was named Fort Emmanuel (Emmanuel *ko'tta*) in 1503 and from then on, the place came to be known as Fort Kochi. The fort served as the bastion of the Portuguese and it extended from the present Bastion Bungalow up to the southern end of the beach where INS Dronacharya begins. At first the Dutch and later the British had destroyed the major portion of the fort including its walls and bastions. Now the remnants of this formidable fort lie submerged. Interestingly, fort Emmanuel of Kochi was the first fort on Indian soil to be built by the colonial rulers. My eldest brother Siva Prasad, an octogenarian, shares vague memories of the dilapidated remnants of Fort Emmanuel which he had seen when he visited Fort Kochi more than seven decades back as a primary school student. The Portuguese ruled Fort Kochi for 160 years. Later in 1683 the Dutch conquered the land and destroyed many of the structures built by the

Portuguese. Fort Kochi was under Dutch rule for 112 years, till 1795, when the British defeated them and took control of Fort Kochi, which they ruled till India became independent in 1947.

Fort Kochi has been famously bestowed with many appellatory monikers by her colonial masters. The British called her "Mini England", while the Portuguese "Lovely Lisbon", and the Dutch, "Homely Holland".

During the colonial period, the twin towns of Mattancherry and Fort Kochi became popular with the former as a vibrant business center and also for the Jewish settlement and synagogue and the latter for its magnificent European architecture. In those days Mattancherry was a bustling trade hub famed for the trade of spices, hill produce, coir, and seafood. The narrow lane leading from Jew Street in Mattancherry to Calvatty in Fort Kochi was dotted with numerous godowns of gigantic sizes. "*Paandika saala*" as these colossal brick-walled, tile-roofed buildings were then called, were used for storing spices, coir, and other such products which were brought there in *Kettuvallam*, the large wooden boats. From there, those products were packed and exported to destinations such as Rangoon and Colombo by ships from Cochin port. The whole bazaar had been lively throughout and the roads and by lanes crowded. While Fort Kochi, just a mile away painted a different picture - a silent and serene landscape by the seaside. As one moved, the din and bustle of Mattancherry gave way to calmness and quietude at Fort Kochi.

The landmark buildings of Fort Kochi include the David Hall, Bastian Bungalow, Koder House, Vasco House, Thakur House, Old Harbor House, Brunton Boatyard, Aspinwall House, Old Lighthouse Bristow Hotel, Delta Study, Bishop's House, Britto School, Cochin Club, St Francis Church, Santacruz Basilica Cathedral, Fort Kochi Post Office and the ancestral home of the legendary singer Yesudas. The entire heritage town has a pretty and fabulous setting with long beaches and a calm and salubrious atmosphere.

Built in 1695 by the Dutch East India Company, David Hall is an ancient building that is a fine example of typical Dutch architecture. The building is characterized by heavy, 3-foot-wide walls and four-column windows buttressed with heavy wooden horizontal beams which support the elegant wooden roof. It was the official residence of the Dutch Governor Hendrik Adriaan Van Rheede tot Drakestein, better known for his *Hortus Malabaricus*, a botanical treatise. However, the building inherited the name from its later occupant, David Koder.

The 18th century Koder House remains the architectural landmark of Fort Kochi across the newly constructed Kochi Water Metro jetty, near Nehru Park. It was in this magnificent building that Samuel Koder, an illustrious businessman and philanthropist who had made many important contributions to the socio-cultural and educational spheres of Kochi, lived. The red-colored, majestic building with its spacious rooms and elegantly decorated rooms with terra cotta floors, opulent interiors, ancient carved wooden furniture, and exuberant wooden ceilings stood out as architectural opulence which adds up to the old-world charm of the heritage town. It was here that the visiting Jewish lords used to stay when they visited Kerala.

Old Light House Bristow House is a colonial-era building in Fort Kochi. This splendid building was the official residence of Robert Bristow, the architect of Willingdon Island, which also has a lighthouse from where Bristow used to watch the ships entering the Kochi backwaters. Later in the eighties, this beautiful building by the seaside had been converted into a heritage hotel, Bristow's Bistro, which attracts tourists from India and abroad.

Brunton Boatyard, located at Kamaala Kadavu, near the Ro-Ro jetty, was a British-era boatyard, where it was said that the British constructed ships for warfare during the World War II. In the post-independence days, the yard remained abandoned for many years until it was recreated to its former glory and repurposed into a heritage hotel by CGH Earth Group. The building boasts of long, roofed corridors, and capacious rooms with high wooden ceilings. The Brunton Boat Yard provides a breathtaking panoramic view of the sea with the spectacular sight of sunset on one side and a captivating view of the modern bustling city with skyscrapers on the other.

Vasco House is one of the oldest residential buildings in Fort Kochi, built by the Portuguese in the mid-18th century. Vasco da Gama was believed to live in this august bungalow. Built in the typical Portuguese architecture, it is one of the most photographed buildings in Fort Kochi and has figured in many films. The large glass-paneled windows and the beautiful balcony add to the grandeur of the building which had been converted into a homestay.

Bastion Bungalow, built by the Dutch in 1667, is another prominent heritage building in Fort Kochi. The building has shot to fame with Kochi-Muziris Biennale for which the ancient building is an important venue.

The Aspinwall House stands as a grand colonial edifice, steeped in a rich historical legacy. It was the brainchild of John H Aspinwall, the chief of Aspinwall & Company who constructed it in 1857. The building was used as the office of Aspinwall and Company which was engaged in the trade of various spices, coconut, coir, coffee, tea and rubber. However, the entire structure was destroyed in the great fire in 1889. The existing structure was built in 1890. Now the splendid building is owned by DLF and the Kerala government has taken on lease which is one of the venues for Kochi Biennale.

St. Francis church is one of the oldest European churches in India established in 1503. Originally a wooden structure, the building was later strengthened with bricks and mortar. The church is a fine example of European architecture with Persian style facade. Inside the church, there is only a cross which is conspicuous by the absence of idols. The old fan made of cloth is still in working condition. When Vasco da Gama died in Kochi in 1524 his body was buried in the church but 14 years later his son took the mortal remains of Gama to Lisbon and interred there. However, the empty tomb of Vasco da Gama is still preserved in the church which is visited by thousands every year.

Santa Cruz Basilica was constructed in 1500 by the first Portuguese Viceroy Dom Francisco de Almeida after getting permission from the Cochin Raja. The foundation stone was laid on May 3, 1505, the feast day of the 'invention of the Holy Cross' and hence the church was named Santa Cruz. In 1984 Pope John Paul II raised the status of Santa Cruz Cathedral to Basilica in consideration of its antiquity.

Pepper House is a colonial era building that was once used as a godown for storing spices. Now the heritage building is used as the main venue of the Kochi-Muziris Biennale.

The ancestral home of Augustin Joseph, father of celebrated singer Yesudas and a close friend of my father at St. Sebastian's School, is located close to St. Francis Church. Recently the building has been vastly modified by its new owners and converted into a restaurant, but retaining its old-world beauty.

The Dutch cemetery consecrated in 1724 is the oldest European cemetery in the country where more than one hundred people of Dutch and British origin are in eternal slumber inside their tombs.

As we come to Mattancherry, the ancient Mattancherry Palace, also known by its more familiar name as the Dutch Palace and the Jewish Synagogue welcome the visitors. Mattancherry is indeed a microcosm of India as people from several states with differing cultures, traditions and languages cohabit in perfect harmony and peace. Where else can you find a place where people from different states come and live together?

Fort Kochi is quintessentially an ancient land steeped in history with many centuries' old heritage buildings - the only heritage site of its kind in the country. It, indeed, is a country within a country straddling boundary.

53. *Chaya* And *Kadi*- A Nostalgic Journey Through Kerala's Evening Snacks

Sipping a hot, boiling tea with a thick layer of aromatic froth in the evening is an integral part of the routine of an average Keralite. One cannot imagine an evening enriched with *chaya* and *kadi*. Broadly classified as *"kadi"*, the evening snacks include a wide array of tongue-tinkling finger foods which together with the hot brew form a gorgeous combination.

"Kattan Chaya", the black tea and *parippu vada*, the lentil fritters are perhaps the ubiquitous and most popular combination among the *chaya* & *kadi* genre. In our childhood days, Amma used to prepare several snacks to be served along with evening tea. Tubers like *kaachil*, *chembu*, and *kappa* were available in almost all households in the modest kitchen garden. The conventional snacks would be boiled tapioca with hot chutney of green chilies or it's slightly modified version in which the tapioca would be chopped into small pieces and would be cooked with grated coconut sprinkled with mustard seeds, green chili pieces, and curry leaves to make a somewhat semi-solid preparation. Some days we would have boiled purple yam, (*kaachil*). In the absence of these items, Amma would serve

boiled bananas sliced into small pieces topped with a thick layer of ghee and sugar.

On certain days, we would enjoy *'pidi,'* which are rice dumplings made from rice flour. On rare occasions, we would have a refined and sweet variant, *Kozhukkatta*, the sweet dumplings, where the rice balls would be stuffed with a mixture of melted jaggery and grated coconut. When the rice flour dough is spread on a piece of banana leaf, filled with the sweet mixture of jaggery and coconut then carefully folded, followed by steaming it would be transformed into Ela Ada.

Back then *Porichunda* was a greatly favored evening snack that had a distinctive flavor and tastefulness. It was a fried food item, the size of a lemon made of tapioca flour, mixed with salt and other seasonings. The outer surface of *Porichunda* would be a bit hard though the core would be spongy and soft enough to be savored. In those days, a boy in the neighborhood used to sell it during the evening hours. While frying *Porichunda* Amma would warn my eldest sister to be careful because as the raw ball would be put into the boiling coconut oil, it would explode causing the hot oil to splash. Sadly, this tasty finger food had almost vanished from the foodscape of Kerala much to the disappointment of our generation. During festive occasions, Amma assisted by her three daughters would make utterly luscious *Neyyappam* or its miniature version of *Unniappam*. Since in those times, there were no fridges to keep them, their usefulness was limited to a few days beyond which they would develop a rancid odor.

Yet another yummy and delicious finger food of yore was *Avalose Podi* and its sweet variant of *Avalosunda*. *Avalose podi* is made by mixing rice flour and grated coconut in equal measure manually, adding jeera and the mixture is then roasted under low flame for a long. It's a traditional and popular snack in Kerala. The healthy *Avalose Podi* is usually eaten with banana or alone sprinkled with sugar. *Avalosunda* is the sweet avatar of

Avalose Podi when it is soaked in jaggery syrup and made into small balls. Yet another finger food that we used to eat was the *Ariyunda* which was prepared by roasting parboiled rice and then grinding it into powder. The rice powder was then mixed with jaggery syrup and a few cumin seeds which were then molded into small *unda*, the rice balls.

During vacation my second sister, who was a master chef, used to prepare diamond cuts. It was made from *maida* flour the same way chapathy was made which was then cut into small diamond-shaped pieces. This would be flash fried in coconut oil and then would be coated with sugar syrup. We relished this crunchy munchy tidbit during our breaks in between the childhood games. During the festival seasons, Amma always expected guests and to treat those guests who came unannounced, she would always keep ready some items like *Murukku*, *Achappam*, and *Pakkavada*. Only items like halwa, mixture, and sweets we purchased from shops, all other snacks would be home-made. Amma's cornucopia would have some of these delectable snacks that used to make our evenings tasty and worth relishing.

54. Fathers' Day Thoughts

This morning as I was sipping my morning tea, I have been ruminating on the importance of Father's Day. The cool and serene atmosphere after a night-long rain provided an ideal mood for such an exercise. A search in Google (our modern-day guru) reveals that the third Sunday of June is celebrated globally as Father's Day, a day to celebrate fatherhood and acknowledge their selfless contributions to the family. I was further enlightened on the origin of Father's Day by Google. The story says that Father's Day is the brainchild of Sonora Smart Dodd, a woman in Washington, who is credited with the idea. Her father, a war veteran, brought up her and her five siblings after the untimely death of her mother and she believed that celebrating a day as Father's Day was a fitting tribute to her father.

During my childhood and early adolescence, I had limited opportunities to spend quality time with Achan as he was working in faraway places serving IAF. The only occasions we came together were during his annual leave. My early memories of him were as an unwanted visitor who visited us every year. The way he enforced his military like discipline at home coupled with his serious nature made him an unwelcome guest to me. What worried me most was that because of his serious nature, my neighborhood friends refrained from visiting our home during those days when he was around. The only alternative for me was to go to their houses and engage in village games like hide and seek, *Kuttiyum Kolum, Kallanum Poleesum, Goli,* and similar pastime games which he sternly discouraged. I felt alienated and this increased my psychological distance with him. I was blinded by anger and despair. The only reasons that made his arrival on leave worthy and memorable for me were the new set of dresses he brought for me and the huge collection of biscuits, a few cans of fruit jams, and butter. His attempts to win my confidence were met with stiff resistance from my side. The main reason for my aversion, fear, and awe for Achan was that Amma and my siblings gave me a picture of him as a rude and ruthless person who would scold and punish me for even frivolous reasons. However, during his two months leave our home became lively with lots of visitors from far and wide. He too found time to reciprocate such visits. In later years, when Prasad Chettan and Rajiv Chettan, my two elder brothers, also became a part of the Indian Air Force, the father-son trio used to come together for their annual leave. The days were enlivened by their noisy talks and occasional bursts of laughter which I enjoyed in silence. They spoke endlessly about service stories and their peregrinations traversing different states and different cultures as part of their job. I felt envious of my brothers for the freedom, closeness, and bonhomie they shared with Achan. Their closest friends Dhanappan Chettan and Antony Chettan were a constant presence on those days.

By the time I reached my upper primary, I endeared more with him, and the father-son bond began to flourish. During those years I was an introvert and tried my hardest to avoid interaction with relatives. It was Achan who slowly instilled confidence in me which in later years prepared me to face the harsh realities of life. After retirement, Achan became my guide, companion, and guru.

Today in hindsight I feel privileged to be groomed under his tutelage and for the values and principles he ingrained in me. He constantly encouraged me to learn English and said my education in Malayalam medium was no obstacle to master the English language. When he asked me to write about something in English to improve my linguistic capabilities, I was too shy to oblige him and then I felt it was too farfetched an idea to speak and write in that lingo. On those rare occasions, when he had to travel to the city, he always brought me copies of *The Illustrated Weekly of India* and admonished me to read the magazine and widen my vocabulary by encompassing new words. It was his continuous encouragement and persuasion that gave me the confidence to write articles on topics related to fisheries and publish them in journals. Though he knew nothing of the subjects as they were quite alien to him, he patiently read my manuscripts and suggested corrections and modifications wherever they were needed. He was a voracious reader and had an amazing memory and incredible intellectual acumen. He read *The Hindu* regularly, a habit which endeared me too to the newspaper. He was a Carnatic music enthusiast and made it a nightly ritual to listen to it after dinner before retiring to bed. This often led to skirmishes between us during my school/college days as I preferred film songs and often changed stations which irked Achan. Quite interestingly the game continues even today as Alekh, my grandson, prefers cartoons on YouTube while I surfed channels to my favorite news channels.

Achan was tempered in the hot furnace of harsh realities. He had a childhood of torments under a step-father who had maltreated him for the sake of his children. Bitter experiences in his early life might have alchemized him into a strong person and enabled him to face many unpleasant realities and several hardships in later life with consummate skill and fortitude. He had great determination and unflinching confidence which enabled him to scale pinnacles of success both in his personal life and career. A sure-footed person indeed. He inculcated many virtues like honesty, sincerity, compassion, benevolence, punctuality, frugality, and patriotism in our lives. For me, he was a symbol of moral rectitude and perseverance in abundance. He had great regard for legal niceties. He meant what he said, he did what he said. He was what he was!

My bonding with Achan became stronger by the fag end of his life, especially after my return along with Suvarna, Kiran, and Athira from the house at Nambiapuram owned by in-laws. The fact that by then I too became a father with fatherly responsibilities might have catalyzed my chemistry with him. When he left on 4th March 2002, I lost a pillar of support and a beacon of hope and inspiration.

For a man, his father is his first hero and role model.

*Written on the occasion of Father's Day on 19/06/ 2022.

55. A Village Beyond Caste and Class

We are living in a world where confrontations and communal violence between various religious groups in the name of caste and religion have become the order of the day. The situation in many places in India is worrisome. Hindus and Muslims are living in an atmosphere of mutual hostility and distrust and each view the other with suspicion.

I have been contemplating about my boyhood days in a village, now part of the sprawling city of Kochi. We lived in a part of west Kochi by the seaside where people of different faiths, religions, and traditions lived together in peace and harmony. When Achan bought our present house some 75 years ago there were only a few homes of Hindus in the entire area. The majority of our neighbors were Latin Catholics and a few Muslim families also lived there. Living in a Christian dominated countryside in the late fifties, sixties, and seventies was a joyful experience for us. People kept their religion and faith at a personal level which they never allowed to interfere with our social lives. Interestingly, almost all children belonging to these three religions were taught in SDPY School, an educational institution that started with the blessings of Sree Narayana Guru, the apostle of *Advaitha* philosophy and a great sage of our times. In our school days, we seldom spoke about caste or religion. In fact, we were blissfully ignorant about the communal divide that separated people.

My childhood friends were Rahim, son of Velikkakath Hamza and Pathumma, Kishore, son of Dasan and Padmakshy, and Robert son of Palackal Xavier and Thresia, who lived in our neighborhood. During those days most people lived under perpetual indebtedness and suffered hardships. They struggled to make ends meet. Amma always tried her best to help them either in cash or kindness.

Together we celebrated Onam and Vishnu, we celebrated Christmas and Easter and together we celebrated Ramzan and Bakri Eid. During Onam, Amma would prepare vegetarian *sadya* in large quantities which would be shared with the neighborhood Christian and Muslim families. Likewise, for Christmas, our Christian neighbors would bring *Appam* and stew. During Ramzan the family of Hamza would reciprocate Amma's gesture by presenting us with delicious *Pathiri* and *Irachikkary*.

We celebrated the annual festival of Sree Bhavaneeswara Temple and Vishu in a truly secular way. During the temple festival, it was the prerogative of the neighborhood boys to make arrangements for the *Para vazhipadu*, the offering to the presiding deity for the prosperity and wellness of the family. *Para vazhipadu* involves the ritualistic practice of filling a *para*, the wooden measuring jar, with auspicious materials such as rice, rice flakes, *manjal*, and coins. For *Para* offered in houses, paddy was commonly used. Youngsters, mainly friends of my elder brother, would collect white shining sand from the bottom of our pond, using which the *thara*, a small rectangular platform, would be made in the front courtyard. It would then be decorated with *kuruthola*, the tender palm leaves split lengthwise into several thin splits, which would be hung from coir ropes stretched between long poles on all four sides of the *thara*. The top of the *thara* would be embellished with a white cloth forming a roof. Then they would arrange the polished and glittering *Nilavilakku*, the traditional oil lamp, *kindi*, the goglet made of brass, filled with water with its tail pointed eastward; a hand of banana, and a few lumps of jaggery for the elephant to eat. Camphor and incense sticks would be lighted for the auspicious occasion. The entourage would include the priest, an oracle dressed in red with the scared sword in his hand, and drummers with an elephant paraded by its mahout. *Para vazhipadu* involves filling the *Para* with paddy from an elongated bamboo basket till it is filled to the brim which is usually done by the eldest family member. After this, the oracle would give a pinch of paddy from the filled para as *prasadam*. Men, women, and children from the locality would congregate in our courtyard to witness the elephant wolfing down the banana and jaggery in a single gulp. Another group would accompany them with a basket containing dynamite which would be burst, for which we had to pay extra depending on their number. A few years ago, the government prohibited the parading of elephants for *Desa Para*, recognizing it as a traumatic experience for the animals, which has consequently stripped *Parayeduppu* of its main attraction.

Quite interestingly, the very same team of youngsters of different faiths would transform into a troupe during Christmas and New Year and would stage brief skits in front of the households of financially well-off families. They would perform in front of a stretched bed sheet which provided the backdrop under the light of kerosene lamps. The actors would be all young boys who would appear in female roles too. The drama would be enacted during the twilight hours from Christmas to New Year. Many such troupes from neighboring localities would visit and stage their performances much to the delight of the enthusiastic people.

During Onam, the very same group would perform *Onakkali*, the traditional dance form. Each team would have 10-15 participants. They would line up in a circle with a lighted *Nilavilakku* in the middle and dance to the tune of the song sung by the *Aasaan*, the head of the group, with rhythmic clapping. Hence the dance came to be known as *"Kaikottikkali"* (play by clapping). The songs would be mostly about lores and legends. Men would be clad in white *mundu* and shirts while women would be attired in two-piece cream-coloured *mundu* and *naadan* *("set mundu")* with matching colorful blouses. Young boys and girls would also be used to perform *Onakkali*. People of all ages and genders could partake in this popular dance form. In those days many clubs and cultural organisations used to conduct *Onakkali* competitions.

During Vishu, the same youths would arrange *Vishukkani* on the early morning of Vishu. They would arrange this with a colorful photo or a statue of Lord Krishna decorated with flowers and lights with a readymade *"Kani"* complete with an array of fruits, vegetables, sacred books, new clothes, gold, mirrors, and a lighted oil lamp in a split coconut. The whole thing would be nearly arranged in a large box. On Vishu day, the group would visit each Hindu household with Kani which would be placed near the door in the front to the accompaniment of songs praising Lord Krishna; *"Kanikanum neram Kamala nethrante niramerum manja thukil charthy.."* The loud chorus would make the family members awake and they would see the Kani. Later the eldest family member would offer *vishukkaineettam*, normally a 25 paise coin which would be deposited in a small bowl.

Those were the most enjoyable and vibrant years in our life where the tweens and teens together enjoyed as much as the grownups with unrestrained joy and cheerful bonhomie. Back then life was a celebration for the children and the grown-up as well which we did in the true sense of brotherhood. I wonder whether we will have such great days in the future when we live our lives beyond the confines of caste and religion in God's own country. A casteless society as envisioned by Sree Narayana Guru, the great sage, philosopher, and social reformer.

56. Achan's Autumn Years: A Friendship Woven Through Time

Though Achan had only a few friends during his twilight years he had a deep and enduring and abiding friendship with them. He used to meet them daily in the Palluruthy veli *maidan*. In the years immediately after he retired from the Air Force in the late seventies, he had a group of friends whom he used to meet and chat at the tailor shop of Gangadharan. The regulars included Narayanan Master, Dr Viswambharan, Illickal Natesan, Adv. Balakrishnan, Xavier *Aasan*, and a few others. Sometimes the group gathered in the *Marunnukada* near the bus stop. But during the hot summer days, they usually gathered in front of the statue of Sree Narayana Guru near SDPY School. They discussed everything under the sun ranging from food to football and spirituality to politics. These meetings normally lasted from 5.30 to 7 in the evening. After *deeparadhana* in the Sree Bhavaneeswara Temple, they would part ways. During my vacation following higher secondary school, Achan would borrow several English books for me from Narayanan Master, who boasted an extensive collection in his home library. Later he encouraged me to take membership in Ernakulam Public Library.

Similarly, while pursuing my postgraduate studies at Cochin University, Adv. Balakrishnan, the then Deputy Director of Marine Products Export Development Authority, would kindly provide me with reference books from their library.

Later with the death of Narayanan Master, Achan abruptly stopped his evening congregation at Palluruthy veli and he along with his friends found an alternate place for their evening gathering on an *aalthara* beneath a banyan tree in front of Azhakiyakavu Bhagavathy Temple. A few others also joined the group like Kumara Pillai Master, Krishnan Nair and Kurup. It was a familiar sight for the devotees who visited the temple, of the elders engaged in friendly chats. Occasionally they would have tea and masala dosa from the nearby Rao's Restaurant. He continued his evening stroll despite his fast-failing health till a few days before his death.

He also had a few trusted friends some of them happened to be our relatives too. A remarkable aspect of his friendship was that he continued to visit the families of his friends even after they died. The wives and children of many of his departed friends told me that his occasional visits were a soothing balm for them. In our social life, we never bother to visit a friend's family after his death and we give scant respect to them. This was a rare, very rare quality which he kept until his final days. Once he requested me to take him to his friend Purushothaman's house many years after his death. His wife and children received him with great bonhomie and respect. When his friends one by one bade farewell to life, the news saddened him immensely. He might have felt that his end was too near. During his final days when he was bedridden with stomach cancer, almost all of his friends visited and comforted him. Despite his immense pains, the presence of his friends seemed to revitalize him, bringing a sense of comfort and solace to Achan. My visit to the temple, a few days after his passing, filled me with sorrow; he was no longer there, dressed in his white *mundu* and shirt, umbrella in hand, in the company of his close friends, engaging in conversation with his friends.

He taught us that true friendship is lifelong. He treasured every moment with his friends. He valued and revered friendship and lived a life that he fancied. In this age of virtual relationships, promoted and encouraged by social media platforms, the value of true friendship is worth nurturing. The warmth and depth of his friendship matured and grew richer over time. A real and trustworthy friend is worth a million virtual friends.

"Friendship is always a sweet responsibility, never an opportunity".

Khalil Gibran.

57. On Photography in a Bygone Era

Recently while rummaging through an old steel trunk my cousin got a very old sepia-tinted photograph of our extended family which was shot sometime in the late forties. He posted it in our family WhatsApp group which had triggered an outpouring of nostalgic responses from the elders. It was shot by my mother's uncle Shankoo who was one of the pioneering photographers in our village and his Prabhat Studio was one of the oldest studios in west Kochi. It was housed in a building along the highway opposite St. Sebastian's church at Thoppumpady, which used to be a sort of a landmark back then. We affectionately addressed him as "photographer *Appuppan*". My eldest brother Siva Prasad said that it took around an hour to shoot the picture of close to thirty people including tiny tots, and the elderly; a stupendous task indeed. It was one of those rare occasions when almost the entire extended family had gathered at the *tharavad*, including those settled in Bombay and the occasion was the marriage of my cousin Rajan, son of *Vallyamma* (amma's eldest sister), to Sobha, the eldest daughter of my uncle Narayanan. (In those days, marriages between first cousins, known as '*murapennu*' and '*muracherukkan*,' were prevalent among Kerala Hindus, a practice that was supported and promoted by the patriarchal system.) The family members were arranged in several rows with the children foregrounding in a row. It was shot on the veranda of the old *tharavad* on a sunny day. Many had a bewildered look on their face as they stared at the camera because they were facing the instrument for the first time in their life and for some last time too. And for some, this was the only photograph ever taken in their life. It was shot using a century-old imported field camera with black bellows which had adjustable pleats and the equipment was fixed atop a tripod.

ESVI studio was established much later at Palluruthy by Kamath Master who was the drawing teacher at SDPY School. In the seventies and eighties ESVI studio famed itself as a much sought-after studio of the little town. During our school days, it was ESVI studio which used to take the customary group photos at the end of high school. Once examination results were published, students would throng the studio to take passport-size photos to be affixed on the application for higher education. Only Black and white photos were shot then. The marriages of my sisters were photographed by ESVI studio. When *Ammuma*, my paternal grandmother died in the early seventies, I remember that we shot a couple of photos of the body with the close relatives sitting on a bench behind the corpse. In those days, photo shoot of the dead body was a common practice, especially among Christians.

After taking photos, we were made to wait impatiently for almost a week or more to get the print as developing print in old analog cameras using films was a time-consuming process. Color photography became popular only by the late eighties which was then quite an event.

Till the forties photos were shot using imported cameras mostly from Japan. However, in the early forties, an ingenious idea of making a camera of our own had arisen in the mind of K Karunakaran. Way back in 1946 Padmanabhan Nair, a studio owner and photographer in Alappuzha, approached Kunju Kunju Bhagavathar, father of Karunakaran who used to repair his Veena and Harmonium. Nair believed that since the camera and harmonium had identical bellows, Bhagavathar would be able to fix his camera. The sight of his father repairing the camera had inspired young Karunakaran to create a similar one by himself. It was made of teak wood with leather bellows. The end result was the invention of the field camera comparable to the foreign-made ones in quality and make and that too at a fraction of its price. This is how the famed "Vageeswari" brand camera took shape, which later revolutionized the photographic industry. The charm of photography has been lost in the digital age, and the widespread use of smartphones has further diminished the skill and craftsmanship required to capture a great shot. Photos are windows which open to the past.

58. On the Art of Letter Writing

During my childhood years, my father was serving the Indian Air Force and he had been posted in many Air Force stations across the country. I can still picture my Amma eagerly waiting for his letter which came from destinations unknown to her as such letters invariably carried the identification number of APO (Army Post Office) and the real name of the place was never revealed as per the Defense rules. All letters that we sent to Achan and my two brothers never mentioned the details of the Air Force Station where they were based and instead indicated only the APO numbers such as 56 APO or 99 APO. Later my second brother Rajiv said that 56 APO is the Central Base Post Office at New Delhi and 99 APO the Central Base Post Office at Kolkata. While 99 APOs cover all formations in the eight north-eastern states, West Bengal and Andaman and Nicobar Islands, the rest of the country are covered by 56 APOs. It was through one of his beautifully written letters to Amma, that we came to know about the exciting and amazing news that he had won the President's Award for his meritorious service during the just-concluded India-Pak war of 1972.

In those days it took more than two weeks for a letter to reach Kochi posted from faraway places like Leh. We treated the postman with great reverence and admiration. Back then Achan and my two brothers used to come together for their annual leave as this was the only occasion for the whole family to meet because they would be posted in different stations at different locations. Those days when we were together, we enjoyed heartily. Usually, this would be in March which coincided with the 11-day long festival at Sree Bhavaneeswara Temple. Once they left for their respective stations, Amma used to eagerly wait for the postman for the letters from her husband and two sons. Today, in this digital age where one can talk to anyone anywhere in the world, we cannot even imagine the mental agony Amma has endured while waiting for news from Achan and my brothers. The first letter that we received after their return would be an event after many days of waiting.

My second brother Rajiv, who is a seasoned letter writer, used to send long and superbly written epistles regularly from his camp in the Air Force during his tenure in the force. His elegant and artistic handwriting and exquisite language made his letters wonderful. As someone who had personally taken part in the India-Pak war in 1972 he used to send superbly written missives giving the nuances of the war in great detail. It was in Malayalam that he sent letters to Amma while he used to send letters to Achan in chaste English. I liked his beautiful handwriting as much as I liked his impressive narratives. His letters were eminently readable and refreshing. Immediately after a letter was received, Amma would open it and read the contents in one go as she had been waiting impatiently for his letter. Once she completed her reading and satisfied herself with the well-being of the writer, she would pass it to us for me and my elder sister to read it. While some portions of the letters I would find incomprehensible I would seek the help of my sister for clarification. Those years were undoubtedly the most wonderful in my childhood.

For sending short messages like birthday wishes or wishes to newlywed couples we would use a postcard as it was quite cheap while for conveying important and serious matters as well as for subjects which demanded secrecy, we relied either on inland or post cover.

While sending a reply my mother generously contributed the tail end of the inland for my sister and me to write. We used to write a draft on a piece of paper which was then mercilessly edited by our mother before we copied them at the bottom end and at times even on the folds of the inland letter. Later my sister would write the address in legible letters from a termite-eaten, yellowish-tinted address book. Those were the days when the erstwhile Post and Telegraph Department played a dominant role in bridging the minds of millions across geographical boundaries. Later when the emigration of job seekers to Gulf countries boomed air mail became very commonplace and began to dominate surface mail.

In this age of digital devices, the art of writing letters is on the wane as people prefer to connect through email, WhatsApp, and Facebook which enables one to send instant messages. However, such digitally generated letters and messages lack the warmth and personal touch that a handwritten letter conveys.

59. Ancient Houses of Kerala

Kerala has its unique style of architectural design which was once used for the construction of houses. Almost all the traditional houses have a commonality with respect to the basic structure and facilities. Whether the roof is made of tiles or thatched with coconut fronds, all of them have similarities, in having a small sit-out in the front with half wall or *charupady*, a couple of small rooms on either side of the open sit-out which could be accessed from the sit out, a spacious room in the middle with two medium-sized rooms on either side. Traditional Kerala houses typically featured a long veranda, and on the western side, an area known as the *padinjattini*, which served as a storage room for grains. In the olden days, all houses were built facing east, and this design layout was a hallmark of Kerala's architectural style. The kitchen would normally be on the northern side, somewhat detached from the main building by a small open area. The entire house would be skirted on all four sides by a wraparound open veranda through which one could easily circumambulate the periphery of the whole building. The doors and many windows would be arranged in a straight row which made the building well-lit and airy. Many houses of those days had wide front doors with four-piece wooden shutters, only the top half remaining open while the bottom half would remain closed as a safeguard against toddlers crawling out and also to control access to the interior by outsiders.

However, the magnificent homes of the aristocracy had many additional features like the *ara*, *nilavara* (the cellar), and *machh* (loft) with beautiful carvings all made out of durable and expensive wood such as teak, rosewood, and *Arjili*. While it is believed that the family goddesses, *paradevatha*, was residing in *ara* (attic), the *nilavara* was used as a safe locker where the valuable items owned by the family like gold, silver, cash, and copper ware were kept. There would be a small open courtyard in the middle of the house called *nadumuttam*. Palaces and such imposing buildings would have *nalukettu*. A narrow and steep stairwell would lead to the loft. In the long-ago years, all houses had plinths of considerable height a flight of 5-7 steps led to the floor. The long roofs would slope towards two sides from the center with two intricately carved wooden *mukhappu* (gable) on either side where the roof ended. Some palatial buildings like *mana* inhabited by Namboodiris would have an extension to the front the roof of which ended in large gables and the area beneath would be the *Poomukham*, the sit-out. For mansions there would be outhouses as integral parts on the eastern, northern, and southern areas of the courtyard known as *kizhakkini*, *vadakkini*, and *thekkini*, the names indicative of the respective directions where the outhouse existed. The roofs sloped down from all four sides, which ended in eaves made of tin, which would be attached to the free end of the roof through which rain water percolated down. For awesome *mana*, there would be a huge edifice called *padippura*, rarely with an attached small double-story building referred to as *padippura maalika*, the gatehouse.

There would be a purpose-built well alongside the kitchen with a perennial source of fresh water which would be used for drinking and cooking. Through a small window, the water could be collected from inside the kitchen with a bucket attached to ropes over a pulley.

Almost all ancient houses had a minimum of two ponds, the main one in the *kannimoola*, along the northeastern corner of the courtyard. The water from those ponds would be used for washing clothes, bathing, and gardening. In addition, there would be one or more ponds in the western courtyard, primarily used for "unclean" purposes such as cleaning after defecation. Interestingly, most of the old houses, especially those of the lower and middle classes, lacked toilets. Family members would often defecate in the open ground or a dug-out opening.

The toilet, when there's one, would be located as far away as possible from the main building. This was followed strictly to avoid possible contamination of water in the well and freshwater pond. Bathrooms would be normally a tiny area in a corner that would be covered on all four sides with a small door mostly of thatched coconut fronds or sheets of gunny bags. Those *kulippura*, as they were called, did not have roofs. However, upper-class families had brick-built, tile-roofed bathrooms, and toilets with doors made of tin sheets. Outside the bathroom, there would be a water tank that would be filled with water drawn from the pond. A pipe would be connected to the interior of the bathroom with faucets.

The southwest corners of the courtyard would be earmarked for cow sheds wherein live the cows. A similar structure for keeping firewood would be an integral part of the ancient houses of Kerala.

In a not-too-distant past, Kerala had been home to several such ancient homes called *tharavad* which were the finest examples of the traditional architecture known as *Thachu Sastra*. Those buildings were with tiled roofing, brick walls, a long porch with wooden *charupadi*, a built-in seat, and an interior heavily decorated with woodwork using durable timber like teak and Mahogony. The design and construction of such houses perfectly blended with nature and local climate. Most of them had a central courtyard called *Nadumuttam* where at night in the privacy of the home the inhabitants used to gather and exchange pleasantries. After sunset, the home and the courtyard would be dark and serene. A few kerosene lamps would be kept aglow from which flickering flames along with soot would emanate lighting the interior.

My Amma used to talk about her ancestral home with laterite stone walls, several small rooms, and an attic on the first floor which was connected by a narrow steep wooden stairwell leading from the main hall and a veranda that wrapped around the building. I was told that at one time as many as 26 people from three generations inhabited happily in this not-so-spacious house which was located in the middle of a sprawling compound with a large pond on the north-eastern corner. During the great flood of Malayalam Era 1099 (AD 1924) Amma said that many people from the neighborhood found safety on the loft of the old house where they huddled together. Interestingly, 2024 marks the 100th anniversary of the catastrophic flood that submerged the entire state. The old *tharavad* had been demolished several decades ago and built the present tiled house. The walls of the veranda had been adorned with long lines of sepia-tinted black and white photos of the family down generations. Over time, the house became dilapidated due to long years of neglect by the current owners. Our ancestors built these ancient houses with careful consideration of the climate and surrounding ecosystem, creating structures that not only exuded elegance but also harmonized seamlessly with their environment. Unlike many modern houses that stand out as eyesores, these traditional buildings blended perfectly with their surroundings, reflecting a thoughtful and sustainable approach to architecture. Each one has a story to tell, about a glorious past when generations lived there in an atmosphere of peace and love. Even during the hottest summer months, these old houses remained cool and the atmosphere pristine. With the disintegration of joint families and the patriarchal hegemony such traditional houses were razed to the ground and small concrete houses took their position.

60. Night of the Fireflies

When was the last time you gazed upon a swarm of glowing fireflies? Maybe years back. For the first time in many years recently on a cold night after heavy rain, I spotted a solitary firefly that was glittering in my pitch-dark backyard among the plants. The sight was an enchanting one for me as I was looking at a firefly in full glow after many years. I thought how beautiful was my village, some five decades back before it metamorphosed into a busy city which is what it is today

In the eastern corner of my ancestral land, there was a large pond which at its farthest corner gradually merged with the canal which meandered along the fringes of our compound. The point of confluence of the pond and the canal formed a tiny flat marshy ground surrounded by riparian vegetation and tall grasses. During hot and humid summer evenings we were delighted by the marvelous sight of swarms of fireflies flickering which imparted an ethereal setting to the night sky. We, the children were particularly delighted by the magnificent nightscape as we were fed on innumerable stories about fireflies narrated by our *Ammuma*. All such narratives were interesting, some intriguing while still others awe-inspiring which fired our imaginations. Whenever we saw fireflies all those tales told by grandma came alive in our imagination.

My neighborhood friend Robert was adept at catching those innocent bugs within his cupped palms and then would transfer the helpless beings into a small glass bottle, closing intact with its rubber lid. When kept inside the dark corner of the room, the flies would emit golden light intermittently much to our joy. We enjoyed the sight with wild enthusiasm. In those days when there was no electricity the entire village would be drowned in darkness after nightfall. Amma, however, would scold us for our cruel deed. She would shout, "*eda*, let them free otherwise, they would die". Later we would release them though reluctantly. We gazed in wonderment at the swarms of fireflies glittering in the darkness against an equally dark sky imparting a delightful visual experience.

My closest friend Obby had his house by the side of the lake and the nearby swamp was vegetated with mangroves which was an ideal and safe haven for hundreds of fireflies. On dark summer nights after the new moon, we used to enjoy the amazing sight of the twinkling fireflies. The swarms of sparkling fireflies used to light up dark midsummer skies, a spectacular sight to behold.

But time has brought many inevitable changes in our once beautiful landscape. The pond in my courtyard no longer exists as it was filled up, the canal which used to flow silently along our homestead is no more as it was filled up to construct a village road many years ago, the marsh alongside Obby's house has disappeared long back as encroachments and unauthorized landfilling had taken them away. As the village transforms itself into a small town the whole town is electrified thus the darkness has also been robbed which once provided the best backdrop for the fireflies to display their magical glow. Only very few of them remain now and they waste their marvelous glow in a night sky polluted by intense light. Though we were blessed with many amenities which we did not enjoy till then the development has taken many of the natural wonders away. Rapid development has destroyed all their natural habitats, the dazzling street lights banished darkness forever, the silence of the nights was broken by incessant human intervention, in short, the fireflies slowly disappeared from our landscape. So, the sighting of a lone firefly on that cold rainy night enthralled me and inspired me to write this piece. For the old-timers, the fireflies and their spectacular glow which brightened up their nights in the distant past are part of cherished memories.

Fireflies occupy a dominant role in folklore and fairy tales and many believe them to have mystical, supernatural powers.

Fireflies have an ancestry dating back to 150 million years, and once upon a time they might have shared this planet with dinosaurs. Fireflies enjoy a worldwide presence except in Antarctica and there are over 2000 different species each with its unique features and characteristics. Without exception, they prefer a hot and humid atmosphere. Fireflies produce light through bioluminescence, a chemical reaction. Oxygen combines with luciferin in the presence of an enzyme called luciferase and generates light without any heat. As a rule, males flash every five seconds and females every two seconds to attract their mates.

Quite interestingly, the fireflies are not flies, they are beetles indeed. Today the fireflies are threatened by several factors like habitat loss, light pollution, climate change, and pesticide use. Light pollution has interfered with their mating signals thus impeding their natural reproductive cycle.

It's a sobering reminder that these wonderful creatures of nature are being brought to the verge of extinction by the deleterious effects of man-made devastations. Every year the first weekend of July is celebrated as World Firefly Day, the day is observed to celebrate their beauty and acknowledge their ecological and socio-economic significance while highlighting the myriad challenges they face.

61. Whispers of the Lost: The Silent Tale of our Vanishing Flora

Once upon a time, Kerala, the land of palms and canals, was a lush and vibrant tapestry of greenery, boasting a rich repository of diverse trees and shrubs. The verdant landscape of the state was teeming with an abundance of flora creating a natural paradise of unnatural beauty.

A few decades ago, Kochi's landscape was home to a diverse array of trees dominated by Coconut Palm, Jackfruit, Mango, Indian almond, Rain Tree, Indian Laburnum, Peepal and the like. They grew everywhere, along the fringes of the homestead, lining the village alleys, along the periphery of the dust-filled village roads, in the sprawling grounds of temples and churches, in the sacred groves, and practically in every open space. Those times were rich in biodiversity with different species of trees, plants, and shrubs in every nook and cranny. A plethora of birds, animals, flies, and butterflies populated those trees and shrubs which made our days wonderful.

I belong to another era where we lived amid tropical plants and trees native to the area. Trees like coconut palm , arecanut palm, mango, cashew, jackfruit, tamarind, neem, banyan, black plum (*njaaval*), Alexandria laurel (*punna*), Indian almond (*kadukka*),

Niepa bark tree (*karingotta*), Chinese chaste tree (*karinochi*), Labernum (*kanikkonna*), Gulmohar, Raintree, Copper pod and plants such as spreading Hogweed (*thazhuthama*), Crape jasmine (*nandyarvattam*), Butterfly pea (*shankupushpam*), Pomegranate, bottle brush, Guava (*pera*), wild Asparagus (*sathavari*), white hibiscus *(mandaram)*, Shoe flower plant (*chembarathy*), golden Champ (*chempakam*), holy basil (*Tulsi*) and a lot more. The northern courtyard of our house was indeed a rich repository of different types of medicinal plants that Amma used for the preparation of *Karkkidaka kanji*. Till a couple of decades back Suvarna, my wife used to collect as many as 25 different kinds of plants for preparing *Karkkidaka kanji* from our compound. Herbs like *Muyal cheviyan, Adalodakam, Thazhuthama, Kurunthotty, Karinkuringy, Thumba, Mukkutty, Thiruthaly, Kuzhalvathakodi, Kattu thrithavu, Kayyunyam* and a lot more. Later after the death of my parents, when the family property was divided it became imperative for my eldest brother who inherited the plot, to clear all the vegetation to build new a house for him. Thus, when the house became a reality all those valuable medicinal plants became memories. A huge Malabar tamarind tree (*Kudampuli*) stood in the front yard of Unni *Aasaan*, the village teacher who taught me the basics of language. Beneath the tree, in its shade an idol of *Puliyampally*, the family deity inhabited. *Puliyampally* lived among the exposed roots of the tree enduring the vagaries of the climate. Once a year, the family of *Asaan* celebrated the festival of *Puliyampally* with great fervor. We were told that on the night of the festivities, the stone idol would be dipped in boiling *payasam* and then it would be changed hands among the frenzied devotees. Surprisingly the hot *payasam* didn't burn their palms. Strange indeed are the ways of village life.

There was a huge mango tree in our front courtyard the branches of which canopied the entire courtyard. During summer vacation young boys from around the locality would engage in village games like *kuttiyum kolum* under its cool shade.

A mammoth neem tree existed on the northern side of our compound in the front courtyard of Puthanpurackal *tharavad* in the neighborhood. During summer afternoons the neighborhood women would huddle around under its sprawling canopy and would engage in endless gossip sessions which would continue till evening when children returned from school. During the vacation, in the afternoons, we—the children of the neighborhood —would play village games beneath its welcoming shade. The tree's canopy also served as a popular spot for itinerant village merchants who would offload their merchandise, they would display their wares and conduct brisk business.

There was a big Pomelo tree (*Kumbuloose naranga*) in the backyard of our neighbor Velikkakath Hamza. Since the unusually large citrus fruits were rare and were believed to have medicinal properties, we used to buy them occasionally. Now I have one in my compound which produces pink-colored fruits. We had and even now have a tree of water apple (*champakka*) which bears small, red, pear-shaped fruits which are sweet and tasty. The once ubiquitous *manchady* (crab's eye), the seeds of which were popular among children as a plaything, has completely vanished from our landscape. So is the case with *appuppanthadi*, the woolly pod produced by the Indian Milkweed which enjoyed a sparse distribution in many parts of Kerala. The small seeds are encased in small feather-like structures which help them to float in the air hence the name 'grandpa's beard'.

In our backyard along the perimeter of our compound, a tall Indian mast tree (*arana maram*) stood which provided shelter to many bats. During dark new moon nights Anjalose, an old, respectable man of the neighborhood along with his sons would come for hunting with his gun and a long 4-battery torch. The mast tree in our compound was one of his favorite targets as many bats lived there gleefully unaware of the hunter. The shots from his gun would break the silence of the night. In my younger days, I harbored a deep fear of him, and whenever I refused my evening food Amma would scare me by saying that if I didn't have my supper Anjalose would come and shoot me.

Around the bank of the family pond, there were many plants and trees which together formed a wonderful world. There was a screw pine, adjacent to which on the other side of the fence in the neighborhood courtyard there was a patch of bamboo trees. The bamboo patch provided a haven for a few waterhens (*Kulakkozhi*) who could be seen walking merrily above the carpet formed by the water cabbage in the pond. A few arecanut palms were planted on the fringes of the pond which had leaves (*thanangu*) with unusually large and thick spathes (*Paala* in Malayalam) from which Amma made fans (*visary*) and the fronds we kept for burning during Vishu. *Paala* in those days was also used widely for bathing newborn infants and children in many families. It was a favorite pastime for children to sit in the *paala* while elders would tow them along with the front in the yard. A lone Cacao tree stood as a representative of exotic trees among these native ones. Full of fruits, the Cacao beans were a relished food for the squirrels in the locality. Among those trees, Amma had planted a few pineapple plants. During our study holidays in college, my friends Obby, Unnikrishnan, and I used to engage in combined study on the bank of the pond amid these trees caressed by the gentle breeze, those splendid days remain as the pleasant memories of my teenage lifetime.

Hog plum (*Ambazham*) was a common tree that enjoyed wide presence in the village, the fruits of which were used in curries to enhance its taste.

Pinwheel flower (*Nandhyarvattam*) had a wide distribution in the village the flowers of which were widely used as a medicine for eye infections.

Kuruttu Paala (Ervatamia) was a common plant with a wide distribution. There was one near my home, by the side of the neighborhood pond. Whenever we hurt our feet with occasional pricks with thorns, we applied the latex of *Kuruttu Paala* as a panacea as we believed in its healing power. It did yield a magical cure.

Many Portia trees (*Poovarasu*) and *Murikku* stood along the perimeter of the compound which were the pillars upon which fences were mended. A huge Bael tree (*Koovalam*), considered a sacred tree, stood in a corner on the northern fringe of the land. Amma later gifted the tree to Sree Bhavaneeswara Temple, the Shiva temple in our vicinity where the leaves would be used for making *Koovala maala*, (garland of leaves), and the wood would be used for *homa*. In our southern courtyard, we had trees like Bilimbi and Nellipuli (star gooseberry), which we used as ingredients in many curries. In the front yard of my sister's house at Edappally there was a huge *Nelli* (gooseberry) tree which would be in full bloom during the hot summer months. A *Plavu* is still there in my courtyard though it seldom bears fruits, the common *Chakka*.

Amma had a modest kitchen garden in the backyard where she planted spinach, colocasia, ladies' finger, pumpkin, snake gourd, bitter gourd, and long bean. Trellis made of webbed coir ropes supported by wooden poles were provided for snake gourd, bitter gourd, and long beans over which they spread themselves with their fruits dangling down. A small stone would be tied to the end of the fruit for it to grow vertically downwards to retain its shape. Several greater yams (*Kaachil*) would be planted along the boundary of our homestead by the side of fences at the foot of Portia trees over which they would spread and grow. Within 5-6 months the tuber would attain maximum size. It was indeed a task to extricate the *Kaachil* from underneath the ground which is done by excavating and removing loose soil from all around the tuber. The laborious effort would be accomplished by Amma and my two elder sisters and sometimes Sivan Chettan or Josey Chettan would help them in the task. The harvesting would be usually done on summer afternoons and for a few subsequent days, we would have *puzhungiya Kaachil*, the boiled yam as a snack for evening tea. Amma would cook the yam with a pinch of salt and turmeric powder which had a nice taste. However, we liked the small bulbil which hung down from the tree. The bulbils called *Mekachil* had thick and hairy skin and were tastier than the tuber which we used to roast in the open fire. *Adathappu* called air potato is a distant cousin of the greater yam the fruits of which were produced on the stem which would dangle down from the plant. It is also very tasty and possesses various medicinal properties. Recent studies have revealed that greater yam is a source of antioxidants and has several benefits. We also had a few tapioca trees which would yield slender though tasty tapioca. Guava tree in the front courtyard provided suitable support for Veld Grape (*Changalam paranda*), a perennial creeper with various health benefits and medicinal properties.

Till recently we had a towering *Njaval* (black plum) in the corner of our front courtyard which used to yield a bountiful harvest of black fruits that resembled grapes in color and size. Many people from the locality used to collect fruits and leaves as a remedy for diabetes. Nevertheless, we were forced to cut the tree down a few years ago as its spreading branches brushed against the electric lines.

Till a few decades ago our town had Alexandrian laurel (*Punna* tree) in many places and children used to collect their seeds which they would sell for a pittance. The *Punna* seeds were then widely used for oil extraction which was used in the treatment of psoriasis and eczema. The once ubiquitous Bread fruit (*Kada Plavu*) and Wild Jack (*Anjili)* have completely vanished from the landscape.

Recently I came across an article in *The Hindu* about the Enea Tree Museum which indeed was quite interesting. The park is located in the vicinity of Lake Zurich. Spread over 75000 sq. Km the park is a perfect blend of art, architecture, and science. From time immemorial our ancestors have recognized the importance of trees in supporting and sustaining the ecosystem and they treated the floral wealth as sacred. *Kavus*, the once ubiquitous sacred groves in South India, were miniaturized ecosystems complemented with trees and shrubs along with countless birds, snakes and other animals thriving on them while ponds and puddles serve as perennial sources of water. Myths and legends have been woven around such *Sarpa Kavus* with the prime aim of protecting the forest wealth by bestowing a sacred image on them. Those sacred groves are home to a number of trees and shrubs which had medicinal properties. Fast-paced urbanization has destroyed many of them.

Whenever the name of Vaikom Muhammed Basheer, the master storyteller of Malayalam literature, is mentioned, it evokes the memories of the shirtless writer resting under the famed Mangosteen tree in his easy chair enjoying Saigal from a gramophone. Mangosteen, which is uncommon in Kerala, has been immortalized by the writer, and the tree became as legendary as the literary genius himself who liked sitting under its shade in Beypore, near Kozhikode.

The *Kanjiram (Nux vomica)* tree at Thunjan Parambu at Thiroor is an equally famed one under which Thunjath Ramanujan Ezhuthachan, the Father of Malayalam Language, used to conduct classes for his disciples. It was again sitting under the cool shade of this tree that he has written many of his poems.

Regrettably, all those trees and their lush greenery have long disappeared from our landscape. Kerala, once described as the land of plants and canals, now have neither, as we have wantonly destroyed them with unspeakable brutality.

Anyone who had travelled from Thoppumpady to Palluruthy by the state highway might have been fascinated by the sight of several huge trees on either side with their branches forming a continuous canopy. It was John Master, a great philanthropist and environmentalist who way back in the early forties planted and nurtured the saplings on either side of the road. In recent years, many trees had been pruned to make way for electric lines, a few fell down due to age and gradual decay. It is feared that the widening of the existing road would spell doom for many trees particularly those on the western side of the road.

During a recent drive to Thiruvananthapuram from Kochi, I was appalled by the horrendous sight of thousands of huge pavement trees which once provided a cool canopy over the national highway, being axed to make way for the construction of a new six-lane highway connecting Panvel in Maharashtra to Kanyakumari in Tami Nadu. When this highway, which passes through 5 West Coast states becomes a reality, it is estimated that around 50,000 trees would be axed down. The government should ensure that projects with the potential to damage the environment are accompanied by compensatory afforestation drives to balance the loss of tree wealth. We are the inheritors of invaluable forest resources, and it is our collective responsibility to protect and preserve them for future generations.

62. *The Hindu* and Some Evergreen Memories

In 2018 as *The Hindu* celebrated its 140 years a special edition was published to commemorate the occasion. The information rich write up which enchanted me considerably had details about the beginning, growth, and development of *The Hindu* as the national newspaper. What captured my attention was the piece with photos of the two tiny airplanes used by *The Hindu* to distribute newspapers to different regions of the country.

Perhaps *The Hindu* Group of Publications was the only newspaper in the whole world to employ its fleet of airplanes for newspaper delivery way back in 1960.

The group acquired the fleet in September 1963 for delivering newspapers to faraway destinations in Mysore state and districts of Coimbatore, Madurai, Ramand, Tirunelveli, and Tanjore. The fond readers in these locations used to get their copies around the same time as readers in Madras City, *The Hindu*'s hometown. Later *The Hindu* strengthened its fleet by adding a few Dakotas and a Heron aircraft to distribute newspapers in nearby Kerala and Andhra Pradesh.

I have fond memories as a boy in the mid-sixties of a small Dakota airplane, painted *"The Hindu "*with its insignia prominently on its sides which used to land at the small Naval airstrip at Willingdon Island in Kochi. The sight of the airplane fascinated me as I used to watch it at close quarters from the nearby INS Sanjivani hospital which I visited occasionally along with Amma for my treatment. For the present generation, this may sound incredible.

My relationship with *The Hindu* dates back to the early seventies. During those days people in our locality seldom subscribed to newspapers. Many in the village used the local library. While we subscribed to *The Mathrubhumi* regularly, *The Hindu* would be subscribed only for two months in a year which was the time Achan came on annual leave from the Indian Airforce. Anthappan, the newspaper man would bring the vernacular newspaper early in the morning. But *The Hindu* would reach him only by mid-noon. Since there were only a few subscribers for *The Hindu* newspaper back then in our village, he was reluctant to pedal a couple of kilometers again just to deliver our copy of *The Hindu* after his routine rounds in the morning. Our house was located in the interior of the village almost a mile from the main junction which added to his hesitation. As a solution, Achan suggested he deliver the newspaper to the *Kochanjarickal Peedika* better known as *Marunnu Kada*, a well-known landmark medical shop selling Ayurvedic ingredients and medicines along the side of the highway which was acceptable to Anthappan. *Marunnukaran Muthalaly*, the shop owner was a classmate and close friend of Achan. The shop itself was housed in a small shanty littered with dried roots and parts of medicinal plants. The pungent smell of Ayurvedic medicines always lingered in the air.

It was Achan's routine every evening to walk up to the medical shop after his evening tea and grab the newspaper. Sitting on a wooden bench kept in the front of the shop he would make a quick scan of the paper while exchanging pleasantries with

Muthalaly. Then he would cross the road and sit in the white sugar-like sand in the sprawling Palluruthy Veli ground. The serious part of his reading would take place here which would last till nightfall. The rest of the news he would keep to read leisurely the next morning. From a very young age, Achan encouraged me to read the English newspaper even though I could hardly comprehend much of what I read.

My eldest brother once told me that when the renowned Malayalam actor Satyan died in Madras in the early seventies, it was *The Hindu* who volunteered to airlift his body to Cochin in its flight.

Later when *The Hindu* started it's Coimbatore edition, the newspaper-laden Dakota from Madurai slowly disappeared from Cochin's skyscape but memories are still fresh in the collective memories of the old-timers.

The Hindu has several firsts to its credit: the first newspaper to have a P&T teleprinter, the first Indian newspaper to have arrangements with *The Times, The Manchester Guardian*, and many others, the first newspaper to have its fleet of airplanes, the first to introduce color printing, the first newspaper to have an internet edition and so on.

A newspaper that started with a weekly newspaper on 20th September 1878 and an evening daily in 1889 today *The Hindu* has evolved into one of the largest circulated dailies being published from 21 locations across 11 states of India. Adherence to trust and truthfulness has earned it widespread respect among readers. Through its impartial reportage and independent investigative reports, the newspaper has redefined journalism. During its long journey, the newspaper has been redesigned a couple of times by renowned Mario Garcia. On its 146th year, the newspaper is still evolving as a bellwether of honest journalism.

The Bookend

As I conclude my nostalgic journey, a kaleidoscopic view of a remarkable era unfolds before me, spanning two millennia and two centuries. I hope you've enjoyed this trip down memory lane and that it has stirred fond memories of your own childhood, rekindled the joy and wonder of those special years.

I feel deeply grateful for a wonderful childhood that has shaped me into the person I am today. My childhood was woven from the golden threads of memories, daydreams, hopes, love, laughter, wonders, innocence, imagination, playfulness, joys, curiosity, and the inevitable fears and apprehensions - both real and imagined. These elements have formed the tapestry of my youth, leaving an indelible mark on my life.

www.ingramcontent.com/pod-product-compliance
Lightning Source LLC
LaVergne TN
LVHW041910070526
838199LV00051BA/2565